The Two Margarets

Danger on the Hill

D1464261

Catherine Mackenzie

CF4·K

© Copyright 2002 Catherine Mackenzie
Reprinted 2012
paperback ISBN 978-1-85792-784-9
epub ISBN 978-1-78191-049-8
mobi ISBN 978-1-78191-050-4

Published by
Christian Focus Publications,
Geanies House, Fearn, Ross-shire,
IV20 1TW, Scotland, UK.
www.christianfocus.com
email: info@christianfocus.com

Cover design by Alister MacInnes
Cover illustration by Jeff Anderson
Printed and bound by Nørhaven, Denmark

In memory of
another
Margaret

This book is based on the true story of
two Christian martyrs – Margaret Wilson and
Margaret MacLachlan. Some situations
are fictional or based on fact, but
the large part of the story is based on
events that actually happened to the
Covenanters at that time. The character
of Donald Mackay is fictional, but all other
characters named in this book existed.

Special thanks to Carine Mackenzie,
whose original research and writing
brought the Wigton martyrs
to my attention.

Contents

Danger on the Hill

'Run! Run for your lives!' a young boy screamed. Blood trickled down his face and his breath came in rough gasps as he tried to warn the people in the valley beneath him. The enemy was moments away but nobody heard or took any notice. Again the young boy screamed as he flung himself into the stream and tried to pull himself out the other side. 'Run, everybody! Run! The soldiers are here!'

At the word *soldiers* they all stopped. As the joyful singing of psalms ceased everyone looked to the preacher and the preacher was silent. Young women clutched at children, old men looked around bemused and then a mother grabbed her child and ran. One by one others did the same. A shot was heard, whistling through the air before the thud as it hit the back of the young boy, desperately clambering out of the stream. He was the first to fall that summer's afternoon, but he wasn't the last.

As the first horse cleared the brow of the hill, the preacher stood and watched, horrified at what he saw happening before his eyes. Someone grabbed him from behind and flung him into the stream. A man holding a child stood in the water.

'I've got two bairns here; I can't carry both. Take one and run!' And they did.

Others ran too. Women ran with their children to find safety. Old men and women tried to run but couldn't. They were among the first to die. They were the easiest for the soldiers to pick off. The young people were harder for the soldiers to catch. They ran like deer, sure-footed, fit and fast. But even then some were cornered, helpless prey, and shot where they stood.

Thomas Wilson dragged his two sisters, Margaret and Agnes, away from the gathering to get them out of range of the muskets. The two girls stumbled in the thick, tangled heather. Terror clutched at their throats as they sped past others frantically trying to make their escape. Scrambling up some scree Thomas hid his sisters behind a lichen-covered rock, just big enough for the three of them. The mist seeped down over the hillside, chilling them to the bone. But it meant that at least their part of the mountain was out of vision. The rock was protecting them and the mist was covering them. Thomas felt secure enough to raise his head above the rock edge.

'Margaret, there are soldiers close by but the mist is still thick enough here to keep you hidden. Lie low and keep quiet and you should be fine. I need to go and find some of the others ...'

Before Margaret could protest at his madness and the dangers involved Thomas had blended into the mist and was gone.

Pale-faced, with tears coursing down their cheeks, the two girls lay there, still and silent. In the distance swords slashed the bodies of young and old and screams echoed round the hill top. Margaret couldn't believe that this was happening in the Parish of Penningame. From the top of the mountain on a clear day you could see the edge of Glenvernock land. Glenvernock: her home. Safety.

'I wish I was there now,' she whispered. 'I want to be home. I want to be safe.'

This was supposed to be a gentle, Scottish farming community in the county of Wigton-shire. Massacres and women screaming – it wasn't supposed to be like this. But now a living nightmare had invaded her community.

As the afternoon drew on the killing continued and then, as dusk came, the soldiers turned, tired of their slaughter, and left the hill. Eventually a woman emerged from behind a high rock, clutching a baby. That afternoon she and others had been there, praying, singing psalms and hearing the word of God – now she was looking for the body of her young son, his last words being, 'Run, everybody! Run! The soldiers are here!'

Margaret, seventeen years old, and Agnes, twelve, stumbled across the woman as they emerged from their hiding-place. Agnes saw her place her baby on the grass and stoop over the body of her dead son. A strangled scream retched out of the woman's throat: 'My son! My son! I would have died for thee.'

The two girls stood, shocked and silent. 'How do you comfort grief like this?' Margaret asked herself. Instead she took Agnes' hand and told her to find Thomas, their brother, while she tended to some of the wounded. As Agnes ran through the heather, Margaret looked at her young sister – alive, not a scratch on her and she was thankful. 'How could I have gone and faced our parents if anything had happened to her?'

She felt guilty as she stepped around the corpses. She was one of the few that had escaped, untouched. Then she saw Thomas coming towards her holding Agnes firmly around the shoulders.

'He's alive,' was her first thought, and then, 'what do we do now?'

Agnes asked the same thing, 'What do we do now, Thomas?'

'We go home,' he said quietly.

Margaret nodded her head. There was nothing more to do here. The wounded were being taken home by their families and the dead by mourning relatives. Margaret looked over to where the young boy had lain. A man stood there weeping. The mother, nursing the baby, sat on the rock staring vacantly into the mist.

'How awful to lose your child,' murmured Agnes.

'Yes,' agreed Thomas. 'He was their oldest, a son. They have no sons now. Who knows what the future will bring for them?'

Margaret sighed. To lose any child was a tragedy but in the farming community, to lose an only son meant you lost the future of the family and the farm.

'What will the future bring for them? For any of us?' thought Margaret anxiously as they began the slow descent down the hill.

Glenvernock Farm

News travelled fast in Wigton-shire, particularly when it was bad news. The wounded were being brought down the hill-side under the cover of darkness – only a thin crescent moon shone through the clouds.

'What is it? What's happened?' Mrs Wilson had spotted a neighbour helping a wounded son along the road. She knew something was wrong and ran out of her kitchen onto the main road. 'Who did this?' she demanded. 'Was it the meeting? Tell me it wasn't the meeting!'

'Aye, Mrs Wilson, it was the meeting. The soldiers came down from the brow of the hill, with no warning. They'd killed the look-outs and only the young lad from Bladnoch farm got away to warn us. But he was shot in the back as soon as he shouted the warning.'

'But he was only twelve years old! They're not killing children surely?' As she stared at the wounded bodies and sobbing women, a chill spread through her bones. Before it had just been an inconvenience to have her children attend the Covenanters' meetings … now it was a danger. Thomas and the girls had been up there in the middle of it all. The thought made her sick.

'Did you see my bairns?' she asked the young man before he limped away.

'Aye, I did. They're fine. I've just passed them on the road about a mile back. Margaret and Agnes have been helping some of the wounded.'

And then in the distance she saw them. Thomas, though younger than Margaret, stood a good head and shoulders in height above her. Margaret, young and healthy and with a mind of her own, stood between him and Agnes. And young Agnes, the blonde-haired baby of the family, caught sight of her mother in the distance and began to run – straight into her arms. Mrs Wilson hugged her children and kissed them.

'I don't know what your father is going to say about all of this, but for now I'm just glad to see the three of you home safe and sound.'

From behind the barn door, a taller, broader version of Thomas stood looking at his family. Silent, unyielding, but with an uncertainty about him too, Mr Wilson brushed a hand across his wrinkled forehead. Striding out across the yard, he hitched up his team to an old cart and stopped some people on the road. Soon the worst of the injured were lifted onto the cart and driven home.

When Mr Wilson came home much later that night he looked his wife in the eye. 'They're calling these times the *Killing Years* now,' he said. 'Our children, all three of them, were in the middle of one of the worst blood-baths this parish has ever seen.'

Mrs Wilson fetched her husband some supper and sat down with him at the kitchen table. 'They've all come home alive, Gilbert,' she sighed, laying her hand on his shoulder.

'Yes, but for how long? They're killing twelve-year-old boys. I don't want to bury my children like they will be at Bladnoch farm.' Mr Wilson sighed. 'I know our children are standing against injustice. They say that the king puts himself above God. Our children say one thing and the parish church another.'

'But the slaughter this afternoon tells us something too.' Mrs Wilson let her gaze wander out into the farmyard. The crescent moon still shone through the clouds and its pale light touched the lintel of the barn door. 'Our children say that they support religious freedom and that all they want is to worship God in a simple, biblical way … the others on the hill today were the same. Where is the sense in it? There's no sense in it. There is evil here and there is going to be a lot of pain for those who don't follow the king.'

Mr Wilson interrupted his wife. 'All I want is for my family to be safe. Keeping my children away from swords and soldiers and muskets is the only way I know of keeping them safe.'

'Gilbert, we can't force them. We've let them follow the Covenanters. Margaret says it gives her so much joy when she worships God. She loves to hear the Covenanters preach about salvation. I don't know when I last heard that word preached from a pulpit …'

She paused before adding, 'And after this afternoon, if I'm honest, I'd follow the Covenanters too if I was brave enough.' She stopped and looked at the pale, exhausted face of her husband. 'Come, we're both tired and the children are long since asleep. We've plenty of time to discuss all this in the morning.'

Mr Wilson reached out to grab his wife's hand. 'And we will discuss it. This thing isn't going to go away and if anything it'll get worse before it gets any better.'

Then as Mr Wilson eased himself up out of his chair, Margaret, who had been listening at the door, silently tiptoed up the stairs and quickly slipped underneath the bed-covers.

Sign the Oath!

The following morning Margaret lay curled up in the bed that she shared with Agnes. Agnes had been kicking her again during the night, her legs pummelling her sister under the sheets as if she had been running from a pack of wolves in her dreams. Then Margaret thought, 'Perhaps she was running from soldiers?' Margaret shivered as the thoughts and memories of the day before thrust themselves at her.

Margaret hadn't slept for ages after going to bed. She had heard the cartwheels returning late and the heavy footsteps of her father crossing the threshold. The muttered voices had been quiet at first and then had grown more troubled. Quietly getting out of bed she had snuck down the stairs and over to the kitchen doorway to listen in on the anxious discussion. She knew it wasn't exactly right to do this but she wanted to know if this afternoon's tragedy had changed her parents' opinion of the Covenanters. Margaret was worried in case her parents decided that they should stop their children going to the meetings. She also hoped that perhaps now her parents would realise how evil and wicked the king's men were – and the parish church who supported them.

The meeting yesterday had been so good, before the soldiers came. Margaret loved to hear good Bible preaching and her heart would leap when she sang praises to God. Because of the restrictions and the persecution it wasn't always easy to hold these meetings. They were usually held in quiet, out of the way places where no one would see. 'It's as if I'm living a great big secret,' she thought. 'And the secret is a matter of life or death. Thomas was saying that there are people in the parish who will betray Covenanters just to get a few extra silver coins. In the past, when the authorities found out about us, they would go round arresting people and throwing them in prison. Now they are killing them.'

Margaret trembled at the awful realisation that her life and the lives of her family were in danger. Quickly she jumped out of bed. She was hearing her mother getting the breakfast things ready. Washing her face and hands in the bowl of water by the window she looked out on the new morning. It was bright and fair and the hillside was just as quiet and peaceful as normal. No one would know it had witnessed a massacre yesterday. Margaret felt the knot in her stomach tighten. The stress and horror of the previous day hadn't gone away with the new morning. Margaret suspected that it would be many, many mornings before she would be able to forget yesterday. Perhaps she never would?

After washing, she dressed. Her dark green working dress was covered with a grey apron. She had shoes, sturdy ones, but she only wore them on special occasions. Most of the time Margaret and Agnes walked barefoot round the farmyard and through the fields. As a result their feet were tough and leathery – just as good as a pair of shoes. Before Margaret went downstairs to help with the morning chores she always prayed to God. This morning she prayed to him about something that was bothering her and had been for quite a while.

'Please help our parents to understand what we are doing, Lord. Surely yesterday will show them how the king's ways are not right. I know that loving and following you is the most important thing that we can do. God, I don't want to stop going to the meetings but if my parents forbid me then shouldn't I obey them? Help me, Lord Jesus. Show me what I should do.' Then she silently closed the bedroom door and made her way down the stairs.

Once she was in the kitchen she asked her mother what she wanted her to do.

'There are the eggs to get in, Margaret, if you could do that. I'll get some porridge on the go. Your father will be back in shortly for some food.'

Margaret went out into the farmyard and breathed in the fresh morning air. The cockerel was strutting about and the hens were either pecking for seeds or snuggled up on a nest brooding. Deftly she put her hand into the nests and took out some fresh eggs. Soon she had a good basketful and turned to go back inside. She loved the hen coop, the apple tree, the stable and the whole of the farm. The sycamore trees stood tall and proud by the dry-stone dike and in the distance she heard sheep bleating. They were all the sights and sounds of the country – her home. It was home, but it was also a place where she and her family worked hard and got a good living from the land. God had been good to them. Her parents recognised this and were thankful. Margaret believed they trusted and loved God too. However, their fear controlled them. They followed the king and attended the parish church because they were frightened of what the king and his men would do to them if they didn't. Margaret stood holding the wicker basket and gazed across the fields. The warm sun's rays caressed her face. She thought about how, on mornings like this, you could feel brave about anything ... but then you had to face the rest of the day and reality. These days there were always people who would hurt and harm. There was danger to avoid and now there would be soldiers to run from.

'I remember the text the preacher had a few weeks ago – "Perfect love casts out fear".' Margaret thought for a little to see if she could remember the rest of what the preacher had said. 'Jesus showed us perfect love by dying for us on the cross. He then rose from the dead to show us that we don't need to be afraid of death any more. We just have to trust him. With Jesus beside us there is nothing to fear. He protects us … and at our last breath our souls will be with him in heaven.' Margaret smiled. 'What a beautiful truth the Bible teaches. That is why I have to go to the meetings. The parish minister doesn't teach me about God's love and salvation. He worships King Charles and not King Jesus.'

Margaret placed the eggs on the kitchen table and went to get a broom to sweep the outside step. 'Tomorrow is the Lord's day,' she remembered. 'I hope Mother and Father don't ask us to attend the parish church with them. I think Thomas, Agnes and I should just pray together in the house, or go by ourselves to the wood.'

But as Margaret strode into the kitchen she realised that persuading her parents to let them stay would not be easy. Mr Wilson stood at the foot of the kitchen table, waiting for her.

Margaret knew that her father would want to speak to her first. She was the oldest. She was responsible. Margaret's mother motioned that she should sit down by her father. Quietly, she did so and then looked up into his eyes. They were dark brown, just like Thomas' and on a good day they would twinkle merrily. However, this morning the twinkle was nowhere to be seen. He stood, towering above her with his dark brown eyes, solemn and stern.

'Before I speak to either Thomas or Agnes I wish to speak to you, daughter. You are the eldest of our children, and therefore I expect you to be an example to the others. You should show them how to behave. Your mother and I want to ask you to leave the Covenanters and come with us to the parish church. We want you to stop this behaviour and keep your brother and sister out of trouble. I want to ask you to sever all your ties with these people and to sign the oath.'

Margaret gasped. 'Never! I will never sign that oath! I can't believe that you are asking me to do that. I thought you would ask me to come to the parish church with you, even to stop going to the meetings but I never thought you would ask me to sign the oath. If I sign that it's as good as saying that King Charles is equal to Jesus Christ. The oath says that King Charles is head of the church. The Bible says that the head of the church is Christ and that we should have no other head.'

'Margaret, dear, your father and I are only afraid that the next time you go to one of these meetings it will be the last time. What if it had been you or Agnes who was shot in the back? You are the eldest. You have to remember that Agnes and Thomas follow you.'

Just then the farmyard door swung open and a slightly dishevelled Thomas stood there, beating the mud from off his boots.

'Mother,' he sighed, 'let me answer for myself. It's not Margaret that I follow – it's Christ.'

Mr Wilson walked over to his son and looked him in the eye. 'Well then, what about Agnes? Will the two of you not realise that wherever you go, she goes, and these days that means that you are taking her into danger!'

Margaret cleared her throat and stood nervously at the foot of the table where her father had stood moments before.

'I try to be an example to Thomas and Agnes, Father. I try to show them that Jesus Christ is King of Kings and Lord of Lords. I have tried to show them that following Christ is all that matters. I have not deliberately taken either of them into danger. Any meetings that we have attended, both Thomas and Agnes have always made up their own minds to go there. I myself will not go to the parish church. I will not stop going to the Covenanters' meetings and I will not sign the oath. I can't answer for Thomas and Agnes. Ask them yourselves.'

Mr Wilson let out a very quiet groan and sat down heavily at the table. Thomas and Margaret looked on, shocked at the fear and heartache they could see in their father's eyes. His hand shook as he reached out for a pitcher of water, before gulping some down.

'Very well. Your mother and I decided last night that we would not force you to do anything against your conscience. I have just asked you to do these things because I love you and because I fear for your lives. Will you do one thing for me, Margaret?'

Margaret looked worried. What was he going to ask? 'What is it you want me to do, Father?'

'Be careful … if not for your sake, for your family's. Agnes has just turned twelve years old. Do all that you can to protect her life.'

'I will do all that I can, Father. But you must realise this too. Agnes has her own mind and her own conscience. She is as much part of the Covenanters as I am. You will have to speak to her yourself … but I know what her decision will be.'

And Margaret did. That night Mr Wilson sat again at the kitchen table, dark and sullen-looking. 'Well, Margaret, it appears that you were right. It seems that you know your brother and sister better than I do. Not one of you will agree to attending the parish church. Not even Agnes. When I asked her to stop attending the meetings she wept. I didn't have the heart to ask her to sign the oath.'

Margaret was secretly proud of the stance that her sister had taken. She knew how difficult it could be sometimes to be strong for Jesus. But then Margaret heard a sob. Her mother's face was buried in her apron as she sat on the chair by the stove. Wiping her eyes, she looked towards her husband. 'Oh, my love, what are we to do? Tomorrow is the Lord's day and we will be attending the parish church without our children – again.'

Margaret looked away as Mr Wilson went over to comfort his wife. She hated making her mother feel this way. 'I would go with them to the parish church if I could but I know what God has asked me to do. I must be faithful to him before anyone else,' she told herself. 'Tomorrow is God's day and I won't spend it in a place where his Word isn't obeyed and his name not worshipped.'

The Secret in the Woods

The sound of the cartwheels faded into the distance. Margaret looked on as the wheels trundled and the horses swished their tails. Her mother's black woollen shawl was clasped tightly across her chest. Her father's best shirt stood out sharply against his dark grey coat. It was another Lord's day. Another day of rest. But Margaret didn't feel very rested. The atmosphere in Glenvernock farmhouse that morning had been sharp and edgy. Not pleasant at all.

Margaret sighed as the horses disappeared around the bend. Her parents would have a difficult time explaining the absence of their children. It had been several weeks since any of them had been at church. As she stared at the spot in the road where the horses had turned, and the cart had disappeared from sight, Margaret felt uneasy. How much longer could they keep going like this? So far it had just been raised eyebrows and pointed questions but that was bound to change. Margaret was certain that sooner or later someone would come looking for her. The minister, maybe? Perhaps a court official or some soldiers?

A small hand tucked itself into hers and Margaret turned round to look at her little sister.

'What is it, Agnes?'

'Have they gone?'

'Yes, they've gone.'

'What are we going to do now then?'

Margaret let that question hover on the air for a moment before answering, with a broad smile, 'We're going to go to church!'

'We're going to do what?' Agnes stared, wide-eyed, at her older sister.

'We're going to church,' Margaret repeated, 'The Woodlands church. Haven't you ever been?' Margaret's eyes twinkled merrily and Agnes looked puzzled. 'The Woodlands church is one mile in that direction,' Margaret pointed beyond the barn. 'It's quiet, secluded and has three members: myself, Thomas and you. Now run and wrap up warmly. Remind Thomas to bring that rug with him for us to sit on.'

Excited, Agnes ran inside and dressed warmly with a shawl to wrap around her head. Margaret also wrapped herself up. Even though it was a summer's day, the wind could be chilly as it billowed down from the mountainside. Soon all three of the Wilson children were striding out across the fields to the quiet little woodland which lay tucked in the middle of a deep gully not far from Glenvernock land.

Agnes shivered slightly at the edge of the wood. It was dark and eerie beyond the trees. Thomas laid his arm across her shoulders and teased her slightly. 'This wood is just a tiny wood compared to some of the others I've seen. You've no need to be such a scaredy-cat.'

Agnes sniffed, haughtily. 'I'm not a scaredy-cat,' she said firmly, and with that she walked straight in.

Margaret laughed, 'Wait for us, Agnes!'

Very soon all three were sitting down by a small brook, deep in the middle of the wood. Trees towered above them, their green leaves shimmering in the sunlight. Thomas laid out the rug that he had carried from the farmhouse and they all settled down.

They began with prayer. Thomas asked God to protect them and to guide them. He prayed for their parents and for the family of the young boy at Bladnoch farm. He asked God to forgive him and his sisters for their sins and that they would learn something from the Bible today.

'But we haven't got a Bible,' gasped Agnes when he had finished. 'We didn't take one with us.'

'No, it's too dangerous to go walking across the fields with a Bible. But I wrote down some verses on this piece of paper which Margaret will read. She has a good voice for reading.'

Margaret cleared her throat and began to read from Psalm 46. It was a favourite passage of Scripture for all involved with the Covenanters. As she read it she thought about all their friends who had been at the meeting the other day. She said a silent prayer for the wounded wherever they were.

As the little church of three sat underneath the canopy of leaves, Margaret's clear voice rang out.

'God is our refuge and strength, a very present help in trouble. Therefore we will not fear though the earth be removed, and though the mountains be carried into the midst of the sea; Though the waters roar and be troubled, though the mountains shake with the swelling thereof.

There is a river, the streams whereof shall make glad the city of God, the holy place of the tabernacles of the most High. God is in the midst of her; she shall not be moved: God shall help her, and that right early.

The heathen raged, the kingdoms were moved; he uttered his voice, the earth melted.

The Lord of hosts is with us; the God of Jacob is our refuge.

Come and behold the works of the Lord, what desolations he hath made in the earth. He maketh wars to cease unto the end of the earth; he breaketh the bow and cutteth the spear in sunder; he burneth the chariot in the fire. Be still and know that I am God: I will be exalted among the heathen, I will be exalted in the earth.

The Lord of hosts is with us; the God of Jacob is our refuge.'

After Margaret had finished reading the passage they all sat for a moment, quietly thinking their own thoughts. Agnes looked beyond the tops of the trees to misty hills and the distant mountains.

'It would be very strange to see a mountain cast into the depths of the sea. I would be scared stiff.'

'Yes, that would be very frightening,' agreed Margaret. 'But God would be with you, just as he was with us when the soldiers came. He is with us whenever we need help. I like that verse that says, '*Be still and know that I am God: I will be exalted among the heathen, I will be exalted in the earth. The Lord of hosts is with us; the God of Jacob is our refuge.*' When I am very frightened I whisper that inside my heart, '*Be still and know that I am God.*' It calms me. And then I think of the God of Jacob being my refuge. I imagine that I am running to God and that he will rescue me and save me from danger. Whatever happens I know I am safe with him.'

'But what if they kill us, like they did that little boy?'

'Even in death God is with us. It says that in Psalm 23 – '*Yea, though I walk through the valley of the shadow of death, I will fear no evil: for thou art with me; thy rod and thy staff they comfort me.*' What do these words remind you of, Thomas?' Margaret asked.

'They remind me of what I do most days – looking after sheep. You need a rod and a staff to look after sheep – to keep them on the right road. That's what God does with us. He guides and directs us, even up to our last day on earth. He is always there, telling us where to go and where not to go. You see, in Psalm 23 it starts with the words, '*The Lord is my shepherd.*' David the psalmist is telling us something special about God. He's telling us that he is like a shepherd – that he is our shepherd. When I'm working with the sheep, I look after them; I care for them. I feed them and make sure that if one of them has a sore leg I treat it. God looks after those people who trust and love him. Every day of their lives he will be with them. Even when they are dying, God is there to comfort them. Then, the moment that they leave their bodies behind, their spirits go to be with Christ.'

Agnes thought a little. 'I remember the preacher on the hill speaking about that once. He said that to be with Christ in heaven is far better than being alive on earth.'

'That's right,' Margaret nodded her head in agreement. 'There is no sin there – no heartache or sorrow. There are no enemies or people to be afraid of in heaven. You don't have to be scared of anything. We won't even have to be scared of doing wrong because when we get to heaven we will have been made perfect and sinless. I'm looking forward to that day.' Margaret's eyes shone with longing. 'But most of all I'm longing to meet Jesus face to face. What a beautiful face his face must be. He loves us so much – he loves us and died for us. Such beautiful love and such strength in one person – it's amazing. He's the Son of God, the Saviour of sinners and yet just as human as either you or me sitting here. He has skin, hair, lips, a tongue and two eyes. When his eyes look at you they can look right into your soul and he knows everything about you. And he still loves you … even after all that.'

Thomas then said a final prayer and bundled up the blanket. Together they made their way out of the wood and up the gully. Through the fields they wandered home to Glenvernock. Their parents would be back shortly. It wouldn't be good to be away from home when they both returned from church.

'I hope we go back to the Woodlands church soon,' smiled Agnes.

'So do I,' laughed Margaret, 'So do I.'

A Secret Message

The cart trundled back down the road. The horses whinnied and increased their speed in their eagerness to get home to their stable and some fresh hay. As soon as he heard his father call out, 'Whoa there then, whoa there!' Thomas got up from the table and went out to help him unharness.

Mrs Wilson came into the kitchen, untying her bonnet and then placing her shawl in the drawer of the dresser until next Lord's day.

'How was church, Mother?' Agnes asked quietly. Mrs Wilson didn't reply but gave Agnes some sharp instructions to take out the cold meats from the larder before her father came back in. Agnes hurried off while Margaret lifted a cover off some of the food that was already laid out on the table. Then she went to fill a large jug with some cool well water and placed it on the table. Mrs Wilson stopped what she was doing to look into the eyes of her daughter.

'You may as well know, Margaret, that the minister himself asked after you today. He wants to know why our children are not coming to the parish church. He has heard reports of you and the others. He knows you are involved with the Covenanters.'

A worried frown passed over Margaret's face. Her mother looked annoyed.

'What did you expect, child? Did you think it would remain your secret? If it means that much to you then you won't mind people knowing about it. It seems half the country is crawling with Covenanters these days. But anyway, the minister knows all about it now.'

Mrs Wilson sighed. 'I'm not ashamed of you, Margaret. I'm just worried. Sometimes it just seems foolish to me – that you would risk your life for this – this idea.'

'Mother, it's not just an idea. It's the truth. It's about freedom to read his Word for myself; freedom to follow him. I'd risk anything to keep that. Others want to take it away from me – I won't let them.'

Mrs Wilson looked at Margaret and then turned away, muttering, 'You have a faith and courage then that I don't have.'

Just then the sound of the heavy barn door shutting urged Mrs Wilson to get the last of the few things ready before they sat down to lunch. As it was the Lord's day there was no cooking involved. It was a day of rest and Mrs Wilson and the family made sure that very little work, if any, was done on that day. The animals were fed and cared for, and that was about it.

When Agnes returned from the larder with the cold meats and vegetables, Mr Wilson stood at the top of the table and bowed his head. Solemnly he gave thanks to God for the food they were about to eat and he asked God to bless it.

Then they ate. The rest of the day was quiet and peaceful until evening when the animals needed looking after again. Margaret made the most of these days of rest. It was a time to think. It was a good time to pray or read.

Margaret didn't miss the hustle and bustle. The Lord's day was to be treasured. Too soon it was over and Agnes and Margaret were snuggled up under the quilt. What a week it had been, thought Margaret as her eyes closed. She wouldn't want to live through this one again but then perhaps next week had more troubles to bring. She would just have to trust God to look after her, just as Thomas looked after the sheep in the field. As Margaret thought about the many, many sheep quietly bleating in the field outside her window, her eyelids flickered and she gently fell asleep.

The following morning Margaret and Agnes were elbow-deep in tubs of laundry. It was a fine, blustery day. 'Just right for laundry,' Mrs Wilson said cheerily, as she sent the girls to the well to bring in pail after pail of water. Thomas helped too. Margaret and Agnes scrubbed, rinsed and wrung out the clothes, sheets and table-cloths. The dirty water was then drained away and fresh water brought again from the well. With the early start they had had, the washing was ready for drying after lunch. Margaret and Agnes spread it out on the branches of the old sycamore trees.

Now and again the occasional sycamore seed would get caught in the wind and twirl away into the distance. Agnes loved to watch the seeds and would sometimes throw some up in the air just to watch them spin. Right now, however, neither girl had any time to watch the sycamore seeds as they grappled with the large pile of laundry.

'Make sure Father's shirts are tied firmly,' Margaret instructed Agnes. Margaret grimaced slightly as the wind kept tugging at the wildly flapping sheets. 'Are you sure these sheets are secured? We don't want them blowing away in the wind.'

'Aye, Margaret, I've checked them twice already. Don't worry. They're not going to blow away.'

'That's fine, if you're sure? It's just I don't want to have to do all this again. We've got the ironing tomorrow, then the next day Mother needs us to help with the baking and the day after that we'll be helping Father in the fields. The harvest needs taking in. In fact this whole week is busy. I don't think we'll even have time to go to the end of the road and back – and doing extra washing really would ruin things!'

'All right, I'll check the sheets again. But you're right about this week being busy. I was to go raspberry-picking, but Mother says that this week we're all needed on the farm.'

Just then, as Agnes double-checked the sheets, a shadow flitted across the field in the direction of the house. Margaret stopped to look. Yes, there was someone there, definitely. Agnes stopped to follow her sister's gaze. A hand appeared on top of the stone dike and slowly a head appeared.

'It's the blacksmith's boy; I can tell by that green cap he wears and his shocking finger nails! He bites them,' Agnes tutted.

Margaret walked over to the wall and told the young lad to show himself. There was something about him that made her uneasy.

'What do you think you are doing skulking around here? Why the silence? Have you lost your tongue?'

'I can't be seen speaking to the likes of you,' the little rogue whispered. 'It's dangerous.'

'Don't talk such rubbish,' scolded Agnes.

'It's not rubbish,' he retorted. 'I've heard folks talking about you in the village. They're saying that somebody's going to be paying you a visit soon.'

'We get lots of visitors at Glenvernock. We're a very sociable and hospitable family,' Agnes replied with a sniff.

'That may be, but I hear that the soldiers are rather hard to please these days.'

Margaret had had enough.

'If it's that dangerous why are you sneaking around our farmyard? What's the meaning of all this?'

'Someone's paid me a real piece of silver to pass on a message to you. You're to be careful and to keep watch. Thomas and Agnes too. That's all they said and I can't say any more.'

'Who was this person? What was his name?' Margaret stared the young lad in the face. 'Go on, tell me or I will say that you're just a liar.'

'It was the preacher himself who told me to tell you. Your Covenanter preacher who was chucked out of his church. So there. He's tall and skinny with whiskers on his chin. He heard something and he's warning you to be careful. It's up to you if you listen to him or not!' And with that the young lad legged it back across the field.

As he disappeared over the far wall Agnes snorted in derision, 'I don't care what he says. I say he needs to wash his hands a bit more often.'

Margaret smiled. 'You're so fussy, Agnes. You know what boys are like, and, anyway, I think he was doing us a good turn.'

Agnes held the empty laundry basket against her right hip. 'Perhaps,' she sighed. 'But he wasn't really telling us anything new. We've been spending all our time being careful lately.'

'I know.' Margaret gazed across the field at where the young lad had disappeared. 'All this being careful gets wearisome. It's all this wondering – whom can you trust, whom can't you trust? I don't like it.' Margaret turned to go back into the farmhouse. 'I don't like it at all.'

Danger on the Farm

The following day was spent ironing the laundry with a large black iron, heated in the stove. It was hard work, and by evening, Agnes and Margaret and their mother were exhausted and ready for an early night.

Later on, Thomas and their father came in from checking the animals. The two men were discussing the weather, uncertain about what the next day or so would hold for them.

'It's just that the rain today has made the ground really wet and it might be better to wait to see how things look tomorrow. If the weather improves then the soil will dry out and it will make things easier for the cutting. We haven't started yet and I think it might be better to wait a week or more just to see.'

'Aye. That squall we had today was bad. We'll wait and then start preparing for harvest if the weather is better.'

Mrs Wilson looked at her husband. 'You're probably right. I'm sure the weather will be better by the end of the week. So it looks as if you can go raspberry-picking after all, Agnes.'

Agnes beamed. She loved picking raspberries. Margaret knew that just as many raspberries went into Agnes' mouth as went into her bucket but the thought of sweet, juicy raspberries made her lick her lips too.

Just as supper was being served a whistle was heard from outside. Thomas got up to see who it was that was paying them a visit at this hour. After a few minutes he came back in quite excited.

'It's cousin John come to pay a visit on his way back from Wigton!'

'John!' exclaimed Mrs Wilson, 'How lovely to see you. Come in, come in. How are the family?'

'Thanks, we're all fine. Mother is asking after you too. Is your cough better?'

'Oh, much better. Thank you for asking. But it's been so long since we've seen you. You're looking well.'

Soon all the family news was being swapped and stories told, and the latest farming news exchanged across the kitchen table. Agnes and Margaret wanted to find out about their cousins and the new baby. Mrs Wilson wanted to know when her sister would be coming to visit her.

'I'm afraid that won't be for quite some time, Aunt. She's well and healthy but with the new baby she's very busy as you can imagine. She would love to see you, I'm sure. Could you make a visit to us perhaps?'

Mrs Wilson sighed. 'I don't think so, John. I have to be careful. I've only just recovered from that cough, but perhaps Thomas and the girls could visit? We're not going to start the harvest preparation as soon as we thought.'

Thomas looked at his father and Mr Wilson nodded.

'Well then, I'll take Margaret and Agnes over to John's. I can pick up that pig he's been keeping for us.'

'Excellent,' Mrs Wilson exclaimed. 'I've knitted a shawl for the new baby so you can take that too.'

Soon plans were being made and instructions given for the journey the following day. John bedded down in Thomas' room and very early the next morning they all ate breakfast and the young people set off with the cart.

Margaret and Agnes sang songs as the cart trundled along the road. Mrs Wilson waved as they disappeared over the hill and then returned to the kitchen to start her chores.

Halfway through the morning she sat down for a bite of oatcake and a small drink of milk. There was no sound of laughing or joking from the girls. No sound of running footsteps or clumping boots coming in from the yard.

'Never mind,' Mrs Wilson said to herself, 'Gilbert will be in soon from the fields but I didn't think the day would be so quiet without the children. I don't think I've heard the sound of another person all day.'

But as soon as that thought had been and gone, hoofbeats sounded in the distance.

'Horses, and lots of them,' thought Mrs Wilson, and wondered who it could be. Straight away she got up from her seat and looked out of the window. A cloud of dust billowed behind a line of six or eight horses cantering down the dirt track to the farm.

Mrs Wilson stood and stared. One visitor was always an event on the farm, but eight at once meant trouble. As the horses drew nearer Mrs Wilson made out the muskets and the glint of steel swords. Soldiers were coming to the farm. A cold sweat broke out across her forehead. Why were these men coming to her farm? Something made her intensely thankful that her children were nowhere near.

A man with tall, leather boots and a thin moustache dismounted from his horse. In his hand he held a scroll of paper; with his other hand he beat upon the farmhouse door.

'Open up! Open up to the king's troops!'

Before Mrs Wilson could get to the door he began to kick at it with his boots.

'Open up, I say, before we break this door down!'

Nervously Mrs Wilson opened the door and looked into two icy eyes. An officer of the king's army stood on her doorstep, cold and arrogant. Mrs Wilson recognised him at once. It was Captain Strachan.

'Mrs Wilson?' Strachan's loud, imperious voice rang out from behind his thin moustache. 'Answer me, woman! Are you Mrs Wilson?'

Clearing her throat she replied, 'Yes sir, I am. How can I help you?'

'Does Margaret Wilson live here?'

'Yes sir, she does ...'

'Bring her out here!'

'I'm sorry sir, I can't do that ...'

'Bring her out here, I say! We have words to say to her, and more than words!'

'But sir, Margaret is not here. She is away ...'

'I do not believe you, woman!' he growled. And raising his arm he motioned to his men to dismount. 'Men, search the house. Search the barn, the yard and the hen coop. Mrs Wilson, we know that your daughter is here ... and we will find her!'

No amount of begging or explanation from Mrs Wilson could change their minds. The soldiers had been told that Margaret was at the farm that day and they were here to get her.

Muddy boots marched through the house. Swords slashed at curtains, doors were slammed. The barn was searched – hay strewn everywhere. When Mr Wilson returned at night the soldiers were still searching. Even the hen coop was scattered to the four winds. The poor hens flapped about confused and frantic. Mrs Wilson ran to her husband, sobbing.

'Gilbert, they're here for Margaret. I told them she's not here, only they won't believe me.'

Mr Wilson quietly whispered to his wife, 'Have you mentioned anything about where the children are?'

His wife shook her head. 'Not a word. They won't listen to anything I say anyway. They are that certain that I am lying and that she is hiding here somewhere.'

Mr Wilson turned to Captain Strachan who was yelling at his men to search the house again. Firmly but quietly, he told the belligerent soldier, 'My daughter is not here. You should have believed my wife and saved yourself and your men a lot of trouble. And now as you have no further business on my property I will have to ask you to leave.'

The arrogant sneer resurfaced as Captain Strachan turned to look at the man who dared to speak to him in this manner. 'We have reason to believe that your daughter is not loyal to his Majesty the King. We believe that she is indeed a traitor. We will leave your property, as you have asked, but rest assured we will be back for young Margaret and your other children. You are under orders to inform us when they return home.'

Then, clutching the scroll of paper in his hand, he re-mounted, ordering his men to do the same, and soon they disappeared.

Mrs Wilson stood shaking uncontrollably, her husband clinging to her.

'I'll get word to them tomorrow. I'll tell them to stay with your sister ...' But just as Mrs Wilson was saying, 'They won't even be safe there,' the sound of cartwheels and a very annoyed pig was heard in the distance. Above the noise of the disgruntled animal, merry laughter rang out through the dusk. Mrs Wilson sobbed, 'Gilbert, what are we going to do?'

'We're going to get them out of here, that's what!' And with that Mr Wilson strode out purposefully down the road to meet the cart and his three young children.

The solemn face of their father and the quiet sobs of their mother soon silenced the laughter. Margaret looked at the state of the yard, the straw blowing in the breeze, the chickens running loose.

'What's happened, Father? What is it?'

'The soldiers have been here, Margaret. They were looking for you. Thomas, get that pig into the barn. Margaret, Agnes – pack your things. You can't stay here. With that pig making so much noise, everyone from here to Newton Stewart will know you've come home. You've got to get away. Your home's not safe anymore.'

There wasn't time for tears. Calmly the girls packed a bundle each, then wrapped up as warmly as they could. As soon as Thomas had packed his belongings, the three young people and their father rode off into the dark.

It would be a long time before any of them came home again – and one of them would never return.

Runaways

Margaret shivered as she held the reins tightly between her hands. Agnes shivered too. Margaret could feel her sister's trembling through the thick woollen plaid she had wrapped round her shoulders. 'It is probably more fear than cold that is causing it,' thought Margaret. Thomas and their father rode on ahead by a few paces. All three horses had now travelled many miles that night and Margaret could feel hers tiring.

Thomas turned his mount round and drew up beside Margaret to whisper in her ear. 'There's a man who lives in a cottage not far from here. He's one of the Covenanters. We can trust him completely. I'm going there now to see if they can shelter us for the night.'

Margaret breathed a sigh of relief. 'Shelter sounds so good. Agnes is shivering here and these horses need to rest.'

'Well, the horses will have to go home with Father. They won't get much rest tonight. Father is going to wait here with you until I get back.' And with that Thomas gently urged his mount down the bank of a nearby stream. Margaret shivered again.

Encouraging the horse to move forward a few steps, Margaret then stood looking up into the face of her father. She wasn't sure if it was the dark shadowy night or the lack of sleep, but as she looked at her father she saw lines and shadows in his face that she hadn't seen before.

As the moon crept out from behind a cloud Mr Wilson directed Margaret to lead the horse under the shadow of a nearby hedge. Agnes moaned slightly as she dozed against Margaret's back.

'Is she all right?' Mr Wilson asked anxiously.

'She's fine. She's tired and a bit cold but she'll be all right,' assured Margaret.

Mr Wilson took off a heavy woollen plaid and gently wrapped it around his youngest daughter. Margaret protested, 'Father, it's cold tonight. You've got to travel home.'

'Aye, and you've got to stay out all night and other nights that will be colder than this. You'll need every scrap of clothing you can get.'

Margaret thanked him. She felt awkward waiting here for Thomas, uncertain of what to say to her father.

'I'm sure it won't be long. We'll be home before you know it.'

Mr Wilson looked into Margaret's eyes.

'I don't think you understand it yet, Margaret. You may never come home. You are in danger if you do.' Mr Wilson rubbed his arms against the cold. 'You may think that you are leaving tonight of your own free will but that's not the truth of it. The law of the land is turning you out and I am too. It's for your own safety that I don't want to see you back at the farm ... not for a long time. If you come back to Glenvernock, I'll make it my duty to turn you out again. If I'm honest I don't think any of us are ever going to be at peace again. Leaving the farm may save your lives, but your mother and I ...' Mr Wilson stopped short and turned away. A tear shone in the moonlight but was quickly wiped away.

Margaret knew then that her father loved them. He didn't often show it, but she knew that he would do anything to save them – even send them away.

Reaching out a hand, she tried to comfort him, 'We'll be all right. Thomas will look after us. You don't need to be frightened. You will be all right with us away. You won't be bothered by the soldiers or the parish church.'

Mr Wilson turned and looked at his daughter, a pained expression on his face. 'Margaret, you're so convinced about your faith, so sure that you are following God's way. And there's something in me that makes me feel that perhaps you are right. But you're still naïve. You're still too trusting. Do you really think that your mother and I will be left alone? I'm certain there won't be a week where Glenvernock isn't visited by either a band of soldiers or a magistrate or official of some description. They won't let up until we either disown you or betray you or pay bribes to the authorities for your freedom. This isn't just about religion or about the monarchy. Greed has been at the bottom of every shooting, execution and imprisonment in this parish.'

Margaret's horse whinnied slightly. Quickly she bent over, running her hand down its neck, soothing it gently.

'Margaret, please listen. Even if you disagree with the Covenanters, you are not safe. All it takes is for a man to have his eye on your fields and your buildings and he'll spin a tale about you and have you turned into the authorities. I've heard that some neighbours don't even bother with that – they just take a gun and use it to get what they want.'

Margaret cast her eyes down, frightened to see the anguish in her father's face.

'Thomas will do his best for you and Agnes, I'm sure, but no one is safe. I'm only just realising this but I'm frightened that you don't yet understand the reality of the danger you are in. Trust no one, Margaret.'

Margaret raised her head and said firmly, 'I trust God.'

Mr Wilson sighed. He knew that. They looked up and saw, in the distance, Thomas making his way down the stream. Another man rode beside him. This would be the last time, for a long time, that he would be able to speak to Margaret on her own.

'I'm just telling you to be canny, girl,' her father warned her. 'Watch your step. Remember that people are people and that you can't be sure of anyone. What your mother and I can't understand is why the soldiers were so certain that you were at the farm. They just wouldn't give up. We told them that you weren't there but they just wouldn't listen. They didn't even think to ask where you really were because they were so sure we were hiding you. Ask yourself, how were the soldiers so certain that you would be here at the farm this week? What made them so convinced? They came to the farm certain that you would be there but you weren't.' Margaret's father stopped to look straight into his daughter's eyes.

'I'm not sure, but I believe you are only alive tonight because we had a change of plans. No one else knew about your trip to cousin John's. It was all too last-minute. You might not be suspicious of anyone, but I am. Soldiers don't raid a farm on a whim. They have to be certain. They were told by someone … someone who knew our plans, or thought they did.'

Something niggled at the back of Margaret's mind. She remembered the discussion in the yard, as the sheets had flapped around them in the wind and the sun had streamed through the branches of the sycamore tree.

'The laundry day!' Margaret gasped to herself. 'Agnes and I discussed our plans on the laundry day and that young lad snuck up on us. He would have heard every word we said. Perhaps he thought there was another silver coin in it for him somewhere?'

Margaret pictured the shifty-looking lad with his green cap and the dirty fingernails.

'But he was barely a child', she thought to herself. Wasn't it a bit silly to suspect children? And besides, that boy said he had spoken to the preacher – surely the preacher knows if someone is to be trusted or not,' Margaret whispered to herself.

As she turned to wave goodbye to her father, who was to return home with the horses, she wondered about whether he was right to be so untrusting of the people in the farms and villages around him. Tired and utterly exhausted, Margaret and Agnes soon stumbled over the threshold of the strange cottage. There was no sound, except for the soft padding of a cat who snuck in behind them and settled itself down in front of the burning embers of the fire. Thomas lay down by the fire so Margaret and Agnes followed suit. The man of the house turned out the light and soon the house was quiet and still.

Margaret fought sleep as she lay curled up beside Agnes. She realised that she didn't know what was going to happen or where she would sleep tomorrow night.

'Lord Jesus, please help us. Look after us. I feel so lost and confused. Only you know what is going to happen … Help me to trust you, whatever happens.'

The three Wilson children had woken up this morning in a different life – a life that was gone for ever now – but she knew that the God who loved her, the Saviour who had died for her on the cross was exactly the same as he had always been. And he was here with her in this unknown cottage just as much as he had been in the Glenvernock farmhouse.

'My life will never be the same but God never changes,' Margaret thought. 'They'll be looking for us now that we're outlaws ... but God knows where they are and he knows where we are. He will keep us safe.' She yawned sleepily.

'But Father was right ... we'll have to be careful ... much more careful ... from now ...'

Margaret's head slumped, her eyes closed. Sleep had won.

Outlaws

'Margaret, Agnes, come on now. It's time to get up. We have to get moving before this man's family wake. The fewer questions the children ask the better. And if they don't see us then they won't let anything slip.'

Agnes looked at Margaret and held her hand, saying nothing. Her face was pale except for the dark circles around her eyes. Margaret looked at Thomas. It was time to go.

Wrapping Agnes in the thick plaid her father had left them, Margaret took a last look at the kitchen they had spent the night in. Even though it had been a strange place the night before, now she didn't want to leave it. But staying wasn't an option so all three gathered up their bundles and set off on foot.

'Do you know where we're going, Thomas?'

'I know where we are going to this morning – a meeting point on the mountain. I have directions. We'll be met there by one of the others.'

'Others?' Margaret was puzzled.

'Yes, we're not the only ones that have had to run for their lives. Some young men from North Galloway had to leave their farm three nights ago. There are others on the hill already. Many have been in hiding for years now.'

'And we're going to meet up with them?'

'Yes, Margaret, and we're going to be living with them for as long as it takes. Don't ask me any more questions because I don't know the answers.'

Margaret kept quiet, even though she desperately wanted to know how Thomas knew these people, how he had gotten in touch with them in the first place, how he knew so much about this fugitive life on the mountains. What was it going to be like?

As they left very early in the morning, they were deep in the middle of the mountains well before the sun had reached its peak. Agnes hadn't uttered a word all morning and Margaret was worried about her. Thomas stopped once or twice to get his bearings and then he exclaimed, 'That's it – we're here.' Margaret looked at where Thomas was pointing but could see nothing. 'There's that rock, in the shape of a horseshoe.'

Now she saw it. The rock was half-way up the slope and it was curved slightly, quite like a horseshoe. 'What do we do now then?'

Thomas looked a bit uncertain. 'There should be a brook near here but I can't see one.'

Margaret turned a complete circle, her eyes searching here and there for any sign of water. But there was nothing. Thomas looked slightly worried. 'We find the brook and then we're supposed to follow it until it forks and we're to follow the left-hand fork up the hill. But I'm not seeing it anywhere. There's the rock, but where's the brook?'

'Perhaps there's another rock somewhere,' Margaret suggested. 'I suppose there could be two horseshoe rocks.'

Thomas looked doubtful and then Agnes said something. 'Listen. Listen.'

They all stopped talking and listened. A bird chirped somewhere among the heather, the wind whistled through the crevices in the rocks and a gentle, moist, tumbling noise seemed to fondle its way down the mountainside.

'It's a brook. I can hear the brook!' gasped Margaret, 'Well done, Agnes!'

Agnes smiled and quickly all three of them ran towards the noise.

It didn't take them long to find the two forks. After taking the left one they travelled on for about an hour. In the distance they saw a cairn. It was tall and dark against the skyline. 'This is it. That's where we're meeting them,' Thomas exclaimed eagerly. And as they drew closer to the cairn a figure emerged from behind it and waved. Thomas smiled with recognition and ran the last few yards to the cairn. He was quickly enfolded in a bear hug. Margaret was surprised. She hadn't realised Thomas was so deeply involved with the outlaws. He had been living a completely different life that none of their family had known about.

The tall stranger stepped back slightly from Thomas and looked straight at her and then at Agnes. 'Welcome Margaret, Agnes. It's good to have you. I'm here to show you the way to the hiding place. Living on the hills is not going to be easy, but I know from Thomas here that his sisters are tough and courageous. You'll be fine.'

Margaret smiled at the gentle, warm face before her. Agnes spoke up for the second time that morning. 'You know our names but we don't know yours. I don't think that's fair.'

'Agnes. Mind your manners,' Margaret admonished.

The gentle face just smiled. 'You're quite right, Agnes. Let me introduce myself. My name is Donald MacKay. Covenanter, outlaw and fugitive, at your service.'

The young man bowed elaborately and Agnes laughed. He looked up mischievously at the two young girls, his dark eyes shining.

'Come on Donald,' Thomas sighed. 'Enough of your fooling around. Margaret and Agnes are both exhausted. We need to get to wherever it is that we're supposed to be going. How far did you say it was from here?'

Thomas cast an anxious eye around the surrounding skyline. Donald stood up straight and pointed east, further into the Galloway hills. 'It's a good three hours' hike before we get to the caves. That's where we stay.'

Margaret tried not to look astonished as she realised that their home from now on would be some caves in the mountains. Agnes held the plaid closer around her neck. The sun was disappearing behind dark and ominous clouds and the first spots of rain were beginning to fall. But there was nothing they could do so Donald led the way east towards the caves.

Three hours later, soaked and shivering, they reached the foot of another dark mountain. Margaret had lost count of how many they had walked past that day. But she couldn't see any caves. However, Thomas and Donald walked on up the hill, so she and Agnes followed.

It wasn't long until they heard the rumble of a large waterfall. Donald started to walk up the stream and then he disappeared. Thomas beckoned Margaret and Agnes to follow. When they got to the spot where Donald had disappeared, Thomas showed them a hole just big enough for a grown man to crawl through. Agnes crouched low and scrambled through, then Margaret, Thomas following close behind.

They crept along on their hands and knees until they turned a corner and a large open space appeared before their eyes. Although the cave was dimly lit by firelight and torches it wasn't as gloomy as she had imagined it would be. Far above them, cracks and crevices in one or two of the rocks let thin streaks of daylight stream down into the caves.

'This is where we are going to live,' Margaret thought to herself, and she smiled.

Men and women stood up to welcome them. A few young children ran around at their feet — and somewhere in the back of the cave a baby cried. A pot of soup was put to the boil on the hearth and soon everyone huddled up close to the fire with a steaming bowl of broth in front of them.

As Margaret stared at her new surroundings she had so many questions she wanted to ask, but right now all she wanted to do was eat and sleep. After her broth was finished an older woman took the girls to a separate area of the cave. 'You can sleep here. It's quiet so you'll have more privacy. If you need anything just ask.'

Margaret realised then that there was something about these people — they were like family. It was as if she had left her home but God had led her to another.

Cave Dwellers

Margaret woke the following morning and yawned. Feeling the strange roughness of heather and straw under her hand, she opened her eyes and then stretched. Of course, she was sleeping in a cave. How could she have forgotten that?

Agnes was already up and trying to get the worst of the straw and heather out of her thick mass of blonde curls. 'Here, let me help,' offered Margaret, teasing a few strands from out of her sister's hair. 'It's difficult to spot some of this straw. It's almost the same colour as your hair. There, I think that's the worst out.'

Agnes then turned and did the same to Margaret's hair. Burnished in the sunshine, it was a shiny hazelnut colour – brown in parts with a copper sheen.

Uncertain about what they should do first, the girls remained seated in their corner. They prayed together quietly before they plucked up the courage to take a peek into the rest of the cave. There didn't seem to be anybody about but then Margaret spotted the woman who had spoken to her last night.

'Good morning, girls,' she smiled when she saw them. 'It's good to see you up and about. Your brother's been up already and he's off with Donald.

They're going fishing. Early morning's the best time, or so I'm told. But you'll be hungry I'm sure. Let me show you where the meal is and you can make some porridge. Then I'll tell you how things get done around here.'

Margaret and Agnes quickly made themselves some porridge and were then shown around the rest of the cave. In the coolest part there was a larder and storage area. There wasn't a lot of food in storage but there was enough and there was cheese and milk and fruit so there was a good variety. Some meat was hanging from a sharp outhanging of rock and some birds were laid out, ready for plucking.

'We're having a treat tonight,' the woman smiled. 'Pigeon – shot in the woods a few nights ago. One or two of the men have muskets here but Donald also has a bow and arrows. He has a good aim. It was he that got these birds; so we will all eat well tonight. We take it in turns amongst the women to do the cooking – you and Agnes will have your turn in a few days' time. We all keep our own areas tidy and take turns at clearing the central area. There are brooms and you'll find any other items you need in this box. We have some children here but they're the responsibility of their mothers. We try and teach them their lessons.' The woman sighed. 'We do our best, but at least these children get taught about God and his Word. Some children don't even get taught that.'

As she picked up a couple of pigeons for plucking she added, 'I just wish the children had some better learning. There are no teachers here. I know some would say that the bairns don't need to go to a fancy school, but I would like it if mine were taught some numbers and history and things like that.'

Agnes smiled. 'I can help out there and so can Margaret. We've had some schooling.'

'Have you now?'

'Yes,' Margaret nodded. 'We could pass some of that on. Are there many children here?'

'No, not many. Just six – three girls and three boys. You could use the Bible that Donald has to teach them some letters, I suppose – but that's all you'll have.'

'That's all we'll need,' concluded Agnes. Later on that afternoon Margaret and Agnes sat together to plan some lessons. The girls loved it and so did the children. When the summer sun was warm and inviting the girls would take the children out from under the feet of their mothers, into the fresh mountain air. There they would sit in the shade of a rock or beside a brook, reciting lessons and working out sums in their heads. An hour or two every day was all the time they could spare, as there were lots of other jobs to do in the caves.

While the summer sunshine lasted, the youngsters were often packed off to scavenge berries or wild mushrooms. The boys would often accompany the men as they searched for wild birds.

But the Lord's day was still the Lord's day despite living in the caves. Margaret was surprised that they could all keep track of the time out in the middle of nowhere. But somehow they had a settled routine and everybody knew when the day of rest came. It actually meant more to Margaret now than it had ever done. It was a link with home. She knew exactly what her parents would be doing on the Lord's day and she would picture them riding off to church in the cart, her mother wearing her best shawl, her father smart in his polished boots and clean shirt. She would then picture them coming home again – to the empty house. It hurt to think of that, so she tried not to picture it for too long.

But for now, the Lord's day was not a day of fearful watching or guilty secrets. Everybody in the caves worshipped God in the same, simple, biblical way. They sang and praised God – telling him that they loved him. There were no frills or expensive extras as there so often were in the parish church.

Someone would read some scriptures from the Bible, they would sing psalms and pray. One or two of the men would try to explain some of the scriptures and help the people to understand a bit more. Donald and the other young men would encourage the people in their faith – reminding them to trust in the Lord Jesus Christ for everything. Jesus would never desert them. Margaret knew this and it was a great comfort to her.

Then, one Lord's day afternoon, Margaret found some time to escape by herself onto the hillside to think about the service she had attended that morning. 'While we were yet sinners, Christ died for us.'

'What an amazing text,' Margaret exclaimed. 'The minister in the parish church doesn't talk about sin or salvation or what it cost Christ to die for us on the cross. The way he goes on about it, it's as though he thinks that everyone who goes to the parish church and follows the king deserves to go to heaven.'

As Margaret sat staring at the clouds, breathing in the fresh mountain air, she thought about the fact that she didn't deserve Jesus' love and that there was nothing she could do to earn his love or forgiveness. 'It was because of my sin that Christ had to die.' This thought sent a chill down her spine. Yet the thought that his death meant that her sin was forgiven warmed her heart. It worried Margaret though, when she thought of her family and friends, attending the parish church, who knew nothing of what Jesus had done on the cross for them. 'They think that everything is all right and that they are on their way to heaven – but if they haven't confessed their sin to Christ and submitted to him as their Lord, they aren't saved ...'

Margaret couldn't help comparing the two situations. The parish church cared more for the king in London and what he wanted and then the little church in the caves worshipped the King of Kings and cared only for what he required. But there were preachers who knew and preached the truth and Margaret remembered the old man who had taught them that day on the hillside. 'It would be good to hear him again and have him answer some of our questions,' thought Margaret. Just then Thomas and Donald scrambled up the hill to join her. She asked the boys if either of them had heard of the whereabouts of the preacher.

Donald screwed up his face, trying to remember the last bit of news that had reached him. 'The last I heard was just before you came. After the massacre he had to hide out for a while, but he managed to get news to some of the others to say that he was safe. I haven't heard anything for a while now. How long have you been here, Thomas?'

Thomas added up some days and weeks on his fingers. 'It's been well over a month now. We're nearly at the end of August. I hope my father got some help for the harvest. He'll find it hard coping on his own.'

'A month?' Donald sat back shaking his head. 'It doesn't feel as long as that, but you're right. I'm a bit surprised then that I haven't heard anything about the preacher in that time. I'm heading off tomorrow to see some folks in Newton Stewart. I'll be gone a week or more. I'll try and find out if there's any news about him then. It's likely that he's been hiding in a barn somewhere.'

Just then Agnes came in on the conversation having huffed and puffed her way up the hill. 'Did you say you're going to Newton Stewart, Donald? Isn't it dangerous?' Agnes looked at Donald who was chewing a blade of grass. She was obviously anxious.

'Don't worry – I can look after myself, Agnes,' Donald smiled mischievously, 'but it's nice to know you care.'

Agnes blushed and Margaret felt for her. Thomas wasn't happy either. 'Donald, we all worry about you going off on these travels of yours. What do we need with places like Newton Stewart? We have everything we need here. Traipsing off like this can only mean trouble in the end.'

Donald's smiling, mischievous face turned dark. 'Right – if that's what you think, tell me what we are going to do in the winter? Had you thought of that? No! We certainly can't stay here. Every winter we have to move out of the caves. Some people can be found a hiding place in attics or barns with more loyal Covenanters and I've got places for most people … Oh but …' Donald faltered.

Margaret looked at his face, trying to read the expressions she saw there. Was it anxiety? Fear? She wasn't sure. Then it suddenly dawned on her.

'He's hiding something from us. What is it, Donald? Spit it out.'

Donald sighed. 'I should have known you'd find me out, but I just didn't want to concern you. I can use all the old contacts from last year – but there isn't any extra room. You can't go back to your parents – it's out of the question. But so far I don't have anywhere else for you to spend the winter. I don't have a place either: one of the young farmer boys has taken my winter hideout. That's the reason I'm spending so much time away. Winter will soon be here. You wouldn't think it on a sunny day like this, but we all know it won't be long. October will be here in a flash and so will the frosts.'

Later, as the young people were preparing to head back to the caves, Margaret spoke to Donald in private. 'We're sorry, Donald, for putting you to this trouble.'

'It's no trouble – honest. And I don't want you girls to get worried. We'll get you somewhere to spend the winter and then, come spring, we'll all be back here – safe and sound.' Donald smiled at her and winked.

'If it's not too dangerous,' Margaret asked, 'try and find out how my parents are. If you're going through Newton Stewart there's bound to be someone who has heard how they're keeping. You see, I worry about them, a little ...'

'And we don't want that, Margaret, my dear. I'll do my best. As you say, someone's bound to have heard something. And if not, then no news is good news.'

Margaret smiled at that turn of phrase.

'I suppose you're right, Donald.'

Bad News

Despite Agnes' continual worrying, the days passed fairly quickly and Donald was soon back at the hearth with the Covenanters.

'What's the news then, Donald? Have you got all the winter places sorted?'

'Have you heard from the preacher?'

'Did you get news of our parents?'

The questions came quick and fast.

'Easy now then, people. First things first. The places are all sorted out. You too,' Donald nodded towards Thomas, Margaret and Agnes. 'They'll be ready for us come the end of October. I've set it up so that I'll take you out in stages. The women with young bairns will go first. They've all got the attic rooms. Then we'll go through the rest of you as we can. We've got the usual barns and outbuildings. And remember, I'm the only one who knows where all of you are. That means if any one of us gets caught you don't know where any others are. It keeps the rest of the group safe.' Everyone nodded in agreement.

'Which brings me to a bit of bad news I'm afraid.' Margaret jumped. Was it her parents?

'It's the preacher.'

'The preacher?' everyone gasped.

'I'm afraid he was captured several weeks ago, not long after the Glenvernock lot here escaped. They reckon that he was betrayed by someone. Apparently he was using some locals to pass messages on. One of them went to the authorities after taking his money and took some more from them in exchange for news of his whereabouts. Right now he's on his way to Edinburgh – to prison ... probably execution.'

The shocked silence was broken only by the crackling flames and the noise of a dog scratching at a flea. Margaret stood gazing into the flames. She couldn't be certain but it seemed very likely: the young boy, the message, the sneaky way he had come up on them and the coincidence of the soldiers arriving on the very day that Margaret, Agnes and Thomas were supposed to have been at home. Her father had been suspicious – perhaps he had been right after all? Margaret had thought he was just being paranoid.

The young boy had passed them a message from the preacher. He had overheard them talking about their plans. There was a strong possibility that the young lad was, in fact, the informant.

Agnes supported Margaret's suspicions, 'That sneaky dirty-fingered little toe-rag!' she snorted. 'I knew he was a little rotter the minute I set eyes on him. Any boy who sneaks about people's farms like he does deserves a good skelping. Next time I see him,

I'll give it to him too – the little traitor.' Agnes' eyes were flashing sparks, but her temper was soon cooled by the rumble of distant thunder.

'It looks like a storm's brewing, everyone.' Agnes hated thunder and lightning. Very soon the fire was damped down and everyone headed for bed. Margaret shivered – the temperature had plummeted. She looked around for Donald but he was nowhere to be seen. She would have to wait until morning now before she found out about her parents.

The next morning she made sure she was up early to be ready to pin Donald down with some questions. However, she wasn't the first, as she discovered Thomas and Donald in the middle of an earnest discussion over the porridge pan.

'… are you sure, Donald? Edinburgh? Why did he have to go there? It's not as if we're living on the farm anymore?'

'Aye, I know … but that's what they said – he had to go to court in Edinburgh. The soldiers have been up and down your farm with a toothcomb. There's not a week when they don't ransack the whole place from top to bottom.'

Neither of them realised that Margaret had overheard them and both looked up, shocked, when they heard her sharp intake of breath. Thomas got up and put his arm round her shoulder. 'I'm sure it's all right. They'll be fine. It sounds worse than it is.'

Margaret sat down beside Donald and looked him straight in the eye. 'Tell me everything, Donald Mackay, and make sure you don't miss anything!'

Donald looked at Thomas who nodded his head. The story went like this. 'Every week, since you've left, your parents have had Captain Strachan and his men paying them visits. That's the polite way to say it, I suppose. They've really been ransacking your father's farm, plundering every last chicken, egg, piece of cheese. Three weeks ago one hundred soldiers arrived at the farm looking for you. Your parents had to feed them, and for that all they got was broken furniture and damaged property. Your father protested at first but that only made it worse. Last week he was ordered to attend the court in Edinburgh. He had to pay considerable sums of money in fines. They charged him with harbouring fugitives, condoning treachery or something, I'm not sure. That's on top of all the other fines he has had to pay.'

'Other fines?' Margaret said weakly.

'The Wigton Courts have been charging him too. Several times since you left he has either had to pay fines to the soldiers when they arrive at the farm or he has had to make the trip into Wigton to settle things there. This winter is going to be hard for them, as it will be for all of us. But the news in the town is that your parents are very nearly bankrupt.'

'Surely not. Our farm is a good farm. We've made a good living in the past. My father's even saved money. It can't all be gone?'

Donald hung his head and muttered something about the soldiers being very efficient at taking other people's goods. 'There have been other people too,' he added. 'I suspect your father has had to pay off some of his neighbours. It's amazing what petty jealousies come to the surface at times like this. I heard a rumour about the blacksmith ordering your father to pay him for work that he hasn't done. Apparently he threatened to tell the authorities that your mother was a Covenanter … but it's just a rumour, mind. I've no proof that it actually happened.'

Thomas frowned, trying to get his head around the whole problem. Then he exclaimed, 'There's the harvest to consider – they're bound to get some money from there.'

Donald slowly shook his head. 'The soldiers took a lot of the supplies. They destroyed a lot of the south field, apparently. The harvest won't be as good this year as it has been in the past … and your father didn't get the help he was promised. Apparently a lot of his so-called friends and neighbours are worried about being seen to help someone associated with the Covenanters.'

'But my father isn't even with the Covenanters. He was against us from the very start. I'd love it if they did join us, but realistically that is never going to happen. It would take something awful to make them change their minds!' Margaret exclaimed.

Margaret then remembered the conversation they had had that night by the hedge. Her father had known the situation better than she had. He had known not to trust even the people across the wall from him. Margaret longed for the freedom to walk into the market square, to visit friends in Wigton and Newton Stewart, to live a normal life. Most of all she longed to run straight home to tell her parents she was sorry for their loss and that she really loved them.

'Oh God,' she questioned silently in her heart, 'sometimes I wonder why we are doing this. And I'm sorry … I know our troubles are nothing to what you have already gone through for us … and it is worth it, I know. Lately, perhaps, I have been taking my freedom for granted. It's just that it hurts to hear about Mother and Father. I sometimes wonder if I'll ever see them again.'

As Margaret sat huddled by the morning fire, the temperature was as cold, if not colder, than yesterday. Just then the fire hissed and spat as a rattling sound echoed around the caves. Margaret looked up at where Thomas was staring.

'Hail stones – that means winter isn't far away.'

Donald tugged his plaid around him a bit tighter. 'Hmm … looks that way. An early winter is all we need. I'm going to have to see if I can get some of the younger families into their winter accommodation sooner rather than later.'

Secret Hide-Out

The following three weeks were taken up with a lot of organisation. Margaret and Agnes said fond farewells to their young students, giving them last-minute instructions as they waved goodbye.

'Remember to obey your parents and keep quiet whenever they tell you. Your lives depend on it.'

'It's only for a few weeks, don't worry. When it is spring again, we'll all be back here in the caves, safe and sound.'

'At least the attic will be warm – not chilly like it is here.'

Then the day came when the last family had left and there was only a handful of older men and women and the youngsters to organise. One by one, people were moved on, Donald taking them to wherever it was they were supposed to be.

Margaret had hoped the early winter was a false alarm. Unfortunately, it wasn't. As the days drew on, the temperatures dropped even further. The food in the larder was very low and Thomas hadn't found any rabbit or pigeon for over a week now. Shivering together in the light of the dim fire, the last remaining Covenanters huddled together to keep warm.

'Where is Donald?' Agnes worried.

'I would like to know,' Thomas sighed. 'If he's in trouble then we're really sunk. He's the only one who knows where we're supposed to go.'

Another three days and three nights passed with the temperature steadily dropping and then one night a noise was heard at the mouth of the cave. A large figure stumbled in, covered in a light dusting of snow. Agnes squealed in delight, 'Donald! You're alive!'

'Of course I'm alive, you wee scamp. Were you breaking your little heart over me? There was no need.'

Agnes blushed again and Donald laughed. Margaret sighed. If there was one thing she didn't like about that mischievous young man, it was the way he was always teasing Agnes. But then he got all serious and Margaret knew that, even though he annoyed her, she owed a lot to him.

Looking towards an old couple on his left and a young man beside them, he gave them instructions to get ready for tomorrow. 'Your place is ready now – wrap up as warmly as you can. The snow outside is not going to ease off.'

Turning towards Thomas and the girls, he smiled. 'I'll be back in three days' time for you lot. We'll be staying together … I'll tell you where we'll be when I get back.'

True to his word, three days later, Donald returned, and the snow was still falling. Their bundles all packed, Thomas, Margaret and Agnes headed out of the cave into the unknown.

'At least Donald seems to know what he's doing,' Margaret thought. 'The snow isn't as heavy as it could be and hopefully by tonight we'll be where we're supposed to be. I just hope it's warm.'

As they stumbled down the slope, Margaret noted that the snow wasn't deep yet, but it was cold on their feet. She was glad that her mother had thought to tell them to pack their winter boots before they had left home all those weeks ago. Margaret would never have thought that she would be away so long.

That night the four young people stumbled through a wood to a clearing where there was an old mill, derelict and abandoned. Donald turned to the others and said, slightly sheepishly, 'Welcome home.'

Margaret swallowed. It certainly wasn't going to be warm. She just hoped that it would be dry... but even that was doubtful with the stream surging past. The old mill wheel was lying on its side in the moss – rotten through.

Thomas wasn't as positive as Margaret. He turned to Donald. 'Is this it? I know it's a roof over our heads but really – look at the holes in it! It's two, three weeks at the most until winter really sets in. How are we supposed to make this place habitable before then?'

Donald sighed, 'We're not on the top floor. We'll leave that part to the spiders. The bottom floor is drier and then there's a small cellar. I'm afraid it was all we could get. The girls can sleep in the cellar as it's warmer. We can sleep in the lean-to beside the kitchen.'

Thomas's dark looks didn't fade when they entered the mill. It didn't just look damp: it smelt damp; it felt damp; it soaked through your bones. In the corner there was a stock of firewood. Margaret leant over to feel it. It was damp … but not too damp, she noted.

'Come on, Thomas. It will take a while but I think we can get a fire going. Agnes, see if there's any flint or a little dry straw to get it started. Donald, I know it's asking a lot but have you thought about food?'

Donald smiled. 'Don't worry. I've got all that sorted. There's oatmeal in the basement and some vegetables. That will do for now. Tomorrow, Thomas and I will try to shoot a rabbit or something.'

Agnes beamed broadly. Despite everything, Donald Mackay was still her hero. Margaret tried to smile too but she knew that this winter was going to be a hard one.

An hour or two later the young people were sitting down by a dim, smouldering fire but it was taking the edge off the cold. A thin gruel was served in a large bowl which they all ate out of. Margaret decided they should save the vegetables for tomorrow. She looked across at Donald. There were questions he still needed to answer … but they would wait. She yawned and turned to Agnes.

'Come on now, we'll clear up and then investigate our new sleeping quarters.'

With that, the two girls cleared away the pot and the bowl and then headed down to the basement.

Huddled beneath their father's plaid they shivered as they listened to the whistle of the wind, its icy grip nipping at their toes and noses. But despite the freezing temperatures the girls slept soundly. Waking up the following morning wasn't so good as stiff bones and aching muscles protested against the cold. Jumping out of bed, Margaret got herself ready. She wanted to find out some things about the mill, about the wood, about their supplies or lack of them and, most importantly, about why they were here at all.

As she crept up the short flight of stairs she came across Thomas and Donald getting ready to head out for some hunting.

'We couldn't sleep any longer in this cold. Thomas has got the fire going again. We kept putting logs on it throughout the night but it still isn't heating very well.'

'Give it time. It's been unused for months, perhaps years,' Margaret pointed out. 'Which reminds me Donald, when you get back I've got a few questions to ask you about this place.'

Donald nodded. 'That's fine. When I get back I'll answer everything that I can. Hopefully, we won't be too long. Pray that God sends us a rabbit or a hare or something.'

Margaret nodded; she would do just that. It was one of their most important needs, food. But now she would turn her attention to the fire. There was a small flame and rather a lot of smoke but it was better than nothing.

Taking some more oatmeal and water she set about making another pan of gruel. She didn't like to call it porridge – without salt and without milk it didn't really taste like what she would call porridge. But it was food and it was nourishment, of sorts, and for that she thanked God.

Further investigations of the mill found various things hidden in cupboards and in boxes. There were spoons, bowls, plates and even an axe in the outbuilding, and a box of fairly dry wood shavings. She left the axe where it was – Donald and Thomas would use that. But the wood-shavings she took into the kitchen. They were a great help in getting the fire going. By the afternoon the kitchen was much warmer and the fire much brighter, which delighted both Thomas and Donald on their return, carrying a rabbit each. Agnes beamed. Margaret got the pan out and all four of them set to skinning the animals to get them ready for the pot.

That evening the rabbits were chopped up and stewing with the vegetables in the pan. They smelt beautiful.

'I don't think we've had a meal as good as this in weeks. We certainly didn't have as many vegetables as this in the caves.' Thomas's tongue smacked his lips in anticipation of the feast in front of him.

'That's right,' agreed Margaret. 'I've been looking around here, and there are one or two things that are going to be useful. There's a good stream for water and plenty of game around. I saw deer today in the distance, and pigeon. There's rabbit, too, of course. Oh yes, and I found an axe in the outbuilding.'

Donald exclaimed, 'I forgot about that! And you must have found the wood-shavings too – that's why the fire's so good.'

Thomas got up immediately and went out to bring the axe in. 'What a find, Margaret! That is going to be great. I thought there might have been one somewhere, when I saw the logs. Tomorrow Donald and I will head out and do some wood-chopping.'

'Before you do that,' Margaret added, 'I've one or two questions to ask.'

'Can it wait until we've finished our supper?' Thomas asked. 'I'm starving.'

So after everyone had eaten their fill and were sitting in front of the fire, Margaret finally got to ask her questions.

'First of all, Donald. Why has the mill been left abandoned like this? Is anyone likely to come by here, and what do we do then?'

'Well, the mill has been empty for years – the Covenanters have been using it on and off as a shelter. That's why you found the axe and wood shavings.'

'But will we be discovered here? Is it safe?'

'It's one of the safest places we have. Nobody comes this way anymore. Some of the more superstitious locals actually believe this place is haunted but most of the people just forget that it's here. There's a new mill over on the other side of the valley. That's what the people use now. This mill was abandoned when the owner and his family fell sick and died. Nobody wanted to take it over after that. So the place was left to go to ruin. It's a shame, but good for us. It means that it's safe!'

Margaret looked at Donald, doubt in her eyes. She knew that Donald was hiding something from them. What could it be this time? Here they were in the mill. It was a struggle, but they had basic provisions. It was safe, in fact the safest place they had ... that was what was wrong.

'You said it was the safest place you had access to. So why are we here? Why not one of the ministers on the run? Why hide three farmer's children in this place? It doesn't make sense.'

Donald sighed and looked over at Thomas. 'Shall I tell them?' Thomas looked doubtful as Margaret spoke up.

'Tell us what? Have you been hiding something from me, Thomas?'

Thomas nodded. 'It's only because I don't want you to worry, but if you know then you'll take extra care... and that's not a bad thing.'

Donald then explained the whole situation.

'A couple of weeks ago when I was dropping off one of the families at a local farm I heard some news from Wigton. The authorities have put a price on your heads – all three of you. Whoever betrays you to the courts will probably get a hefty sum of money as a reward.'

Margaret stared at Thomas, uncertain. 'Surely all the Covenanters have prices on their heads. Why are we special cases?'

'There are three of you! That means a lot of money. And I'm sorry — with all that money on your heads and all that danger, none of our usual contacts were willing to take any of you.'

'Huh!' snorted Agnes. 'You just said there wasn't any room.'

'And that was true. This year has been difficult because there are so many of us. But what is also true — and I'm sorry I didn't tell you — is that the people are afraid. Your names mean trouble, and taking you to the mill was the only option.'

Thomas looked at Margaret. 'I should have told you. I'm sorry. But now, perhaps you'll take extra care?'

Margaret nodded. Her father had said not to trust anyone. As the weeks and months went by it seemed as if he were being proved right. The thought of having a price on her head brought it all sharply into focus. 'Oh God, protect us,' she whispered.

Donald leant over and said urgently, '… and he will protect us.'

Something shivered inside Margaret as she thought, 'Yes … even unto death.'

Danger at the Mill

As the weeks passed something began to concern Margaret. There were still berries and roots to supplement their diet but as the winter drew in Margaret knew that these things would eventually die out. Even though Donald and Thomas were providing meat for the pot they were now having to go further afield to get it. Often they were gone a full day or even longer – searching for signs of rabbit and other animals. As the temperature dropped, hunting was getting harder because animals were now sheltering in burrows or huddled in bushes or trees.

Then the day came when Thomas and Donald came back empty-handed. They stumbled into the mill, a flurry of snow following them, their hands and lips blue from the cold. Thomas muttered something about trying again tomorrow and Margaret shoved a bowl of thin, but warm soup into their hands. They devoured it ravenously.

However, the following day was the same, and the next. The depleted larder got smaller and smaller and Margaret began to worry.

Desperately she prayed to God for help. She knew he was with them. She trusted him in everything.

But as the winter progressed times got even harder. Then, one morning, Margaret awoke to the sounds of moaning from the bed beside her. Agnes was in pain … a lot of pain. She reached over to feel her sister's forehead, as she had seen her mother do on many occasions, and she withdrew her hand in shock. Agnes was burning up.

'She's got a fever!' Margaret thought, in alarm, Quickly, she wrapped Agnes up in as many layers as she could and ran up the stairs to get Thomas.

'Quick, carry Agnes up the stairs. We'll lay her by the fire to keep her warm. Give me your blanket, Thomas. I'll make a bed up for her here.' Thomas ran to get the blanket while Donald dashed down the stairs to carry Agnes up to the fire. Margaret noted how his mischievous teasing stopped when he thought Agnes was in danger. And that was true: she was in danger. The fever was violent and Agnes lay on the bed shaking.

'I know you've tried, but you've got to go hunting again, Thomas,' Margaret urged. 'I need to make good nourishing soup, not this weak broth I've been giving her.'

Thomas nodded. 'We'll try the east side of the wood – we haven't been there for a couple of weeks. Some of the game might have moved back.'

Donald looked doubtful but agreed to try anyway. That night the two young men didn't return, nor the next morning. As Margaret tended to her little sister she kept one eye on the fever and another eye on the door, anxious for their return. The following night, in the middle of one of the worst snow-storms she had ever seen, Donald and Thomas stumbled through the door – empty-handed.

Thomas slumped beside the fire, sobbing. 'We've walked miles, ever since we last saw you. We haven't stopped, but there's nothing … There was a rabbit, but my hands were so cold I missed the shot.' His shoulders shaking, Thomas huddled in the corner. Donald stood by the doorway, tall and dark.

'Come in, Donald – come away from the door. There's nothing you can do now.'

'I won't have it!' he burst out, 'I'm not going to give in like this.'

With that he turned on his heels and headed out into the storm. Margaret yelled to him through the snow, but seconds later there was no sign of him. Hurriedly, she shut the door against the driving blizzard. It felt as if her whole world was falling about her ears. Agnes lay with a raging fever; Thomas was huddled exhausted in the corner; Donald had left them for who knows where; and she was here having to cope with it all. Some hours later the storm abated and Margaret threw more logs on the fire. At least wood was in good supply, though it didn't seem to matter how brightly the fire burned – the cold always found its way into the house, into your bed and into your bones.

She shook Thomas on the shoulder and he woke with a start. 'Thomas, watch Agnes for a while. I'm going out to see if I can find Donald.'

'Be careful, Margaret. Are you sure you should go? He'll find his own way back.'

'I know but I just want to check. There's some meal in the cupboard. If Agnes wakes, try and get her to eat something.'

Wrapped up in the long plaid Margaret tied her boots on tightly and ventured out into the snow. She hadn't told Thomas what she really planned to do. If he had known he would have stopped her because what she was about to do was truly dangerous to herself and the others. It was a big risk. She was going to see if she could get help.

The following day, a small dark figure was seen flitting from farm house to farm house. Many farmers' wives in the area told their husbands about the young beggar woman who had come to their kitchen doors that morning. Some had felt sorry for her and handed her an egg – or a portion of meal. Some felt suspicious of her. 'One of those outlaws probably – hiding out in the woods. It would serve her right if she got caught.'

Margaret ignored the hostility and was thankful for the generosity. As the night drew on she was careful to avoid being seen returning towards the woods. She waited until it was pitch dark and then made her way back, clutching a small bag of provisions. There was no meat and very few vegetables. It seemed that everyone was having a hard winter. However, the little that she did have was more than she had hoped for and quickly she made her way back through the forest. She needed to get home before the blizzard returned. When she arrived back at the mill, though, a smell met her on the wind.

'I must be dreaming. The hunger is making me imagine things ... I'm smelling roast chicken!'

Opening the door to the mill she discovered that her nose had been telling the truth. Donald stood there over the fire, basting a chicken.

'Margaret!' Thomas called out, relieved to see her home safe. 'Where have you been?'

Margaret hung her head. Should she tell them? She looked into Donald's eyes and realised that he already knew where she had been. Silently she sat down by the fire and lay before them the three eggs, handful of meal and vegetables that she had collected.

'Where did you get these, Margaret?' Thomas asked.

Donald coughed and muttered, 'Can't you see she's tired, Thomas? Don't bother her just now. We'll sort it out tomorrow. Cook one of these eggs for Agnes – she might feel like eating now.'

Margaret suddenly remembered she hadn't seen Agnes. She looked up and saw her wrapped up warmly in the lean-to beside the kitchen. The violent flush of fever had subsided and she was sleeping peacefully.

Thomas asked Margaret if he should wake her. Margaret shook her head. 'Leave her for now. Cook that egg later, Thomas. Right now she needs to sleep… she's been through so…' but Margaret couldn't finish her sentence as she began to weep from exhaustion and relief. As a plate of food was placed in front of her she could honestly say she had never felt so thankful. Donald solemnly gave thanks to God for the food before they tucked in. The trauma of the last week gave that simple, profound prayer a totally new meaning for all of them.

The following morning she accompanied Donald into the forest to chop the wood. Before he started chopping they stood together in the early morning frost.

'You know, don't you?' Margaret said quietly.

'Yes, Margaret, I know you were begging. You took a big risk, Margaret, but you had to. I just hope that nobody saw you coming back this way. Some of them would have suspected you were an outlaw.'

'How did you get that chicken, then?' Margaret asked.

Donald shifted uneasily. Margaret gasped, 'You didn't steal it did you?'

'No, of course I didn't steal it. If a chicken wanders along the road, gets lost and then blunders into you when you're walking through the wood – that's not stealing.'

'Was there a farm near by?'

'Not that I could see.'

'Did you look?'

'Yes, I did, Miss Wilson — I looked north and south and east and west and saw no sign of man or building. So I don't care what you say: that chicken was provided for us by God, and it's safe and sound in our pot and bellies.'

Margaret didn't argue with that and as she was just about to turn to go home, she froze on the spot. 'Donald, look!' Just beyond them, emerging from a thicket, was an unusually plump rabbit. Donald swallowed slightly. Then, in one swift, fluid, movement he bent down, picked up his bow and took aim. The arrow whistled as it streaked through the air and then thud — it hit its target. The rabbit leapt in the air and then fell back into the thicket. Margaret breathed a sigh of relief. They didn't need to worry about meals for the next day or so.

'Praise God,' she whispered, her breath clouding on the frosty morning air. Above them the crows cawed and other birds joined in the barrage of sound, warning the other animals that the hunter was in the woods. But Margaret didn't care. They had food now — God had provided for them again.

The Traitor

When the spring finally came, Margaret relished being able to go out and forage for fresh plants to add to the cooking-pot. However, even though the snows were thawing, the prospect of returning to the cave in the mountain was still uncertain. Freak storms could still appear out of nowhere so they would remain in the woods until the weather was more settled.

They still had to ration some of their provisions carefully as the barrel of meal was beginning to run low, amongst other things. 'I can't remember when I last had a glass of milk,' Thomas sighed.

'It would have been the morning we left Glenvernock farm,' Agnes pointed out. Thomas nodded, remembering the warm farm kitchen with its well-stocked larder. There had been no news of their parents over the winter months. Margaret often hoped that Donald's saying, 'No news is good news,' would be true this time … even though it hadn't been in the past.

As the weeks passed, Donald started to go on his travels again. He had to check up on the other Covenanters hiding out in barns and attics over the county. Though Agnes' fever had left her long ago, her health was still weak. On one of his flying visits to the mill, Donald realised that they might have a problem.

Quietly he admitted to Margaret that he was worried about how Agnes would face another winter like the last one.

'Let us cross that bridge when we come to it, Donald,' Margaret insisted. 'It may be that in a year's time things will be different – the crisis might be over and we'll all be allowed to go home.'

Donald sighed. He had thought that the winter and the struggles they had had would wake Margaret up to the reality of the situation. 'You don't realise, do you?' he exclaimed. 'This might end up being a way of life for you... for all of us... and if that is the case we should be thankful. You won't have heard but the preacher was hung on a gibbet in Edinburgh in November. Things aren't getting better, Margaret, just worse.'

Tears pricked the back of Margaret's eyelids as she thought about the tall, solemn figure who had preached to her so many times on the mountain. She remembered the last time she had seen him, running from the hill clutching a child ... and now he was dead. He'd been hung like a criminal on a scaffold in the middle of Edinburgh – to be gawped at by strangers and laughed at by his enemies. These thoughts, however, rang a bell as she remembered another, her Lord and Saviour Jesus Christ, who had been tortured, nailed to a cross, mocked and treated like a criminal, and he had never done anything wrong.

'You love me, Jesus,' Margaret thought, as she realised yet again that it was because of her sins that Jesus had suffered on a cross at Calvary.

One morning Donald flung the mill door open and rushed into the kitchen. Margaret jumped up and Agnes stared at him. He was flushed, excited, as if he had some very important news.

'What is it, Donald?' Agnes asked. 'Why are you back so early? You said you would be away another week.'

Donald's eyes flashed mischievously. Margaret was glad to see the cheeky twinkle back in his eyes, even though it meant that his old teasing nature was probably back too.

'I've heard some news … important news. The king is dead.'

Margaret gasped. That was a shock. 'What does that mean then? Can we go home?' she asked hopefully.

Donald didn't look quite so excited then. 'Sorry, girls but no. Not yet, anyway. Nobody knows how things are going to turn out. The officials are still in charge and there's a new King now. But even though the persecution has died down a bit, we'll still have to go back to the cave when the weather improves. The snow has melted up at the caves so that's why I'm heading up there now – just to sort things out. Thomas will help you get ready to move out and I'll see you up there in a fortnight or so.'

As Donald left again in a hurry, Margaret pondered the earth-shattering news. The persecution had abated; the King was dead. Surely this meant the beginning of good things? Agnes felt so.

Thomas, however, wasn't so sure. 'Donald said we were to head up to the caves as usual in a couple of weeks.'

'I know, Thomas, and we will. But perhaps we don't have to worry so much now. We might even be able to visit the farm before we go up?'

'Not at all, girls. As soon as you're spotted, the soldiers will be paying visits on our parents again. We owe it to them to steer clear of the farm.'

Margaret nodded, but to herself she thought quietly about other alternatives. The prospect of freedom was too exciting to ignore. That night she turned to Agnes in their bed and excitedly made the following suggestion. 'Next week, before we head off to the hills again, we could perhaps make a short trip into Wigton?'

'Will it be safe?' questioned Agnes.

'I think so, if we're careful. For months now I've longed to go and see old Margaret MacLachlan. She's such a loving, wise old Christian woman. It's been too long since I've seen her.'

Agnes nodded, 'I'd love to see her too, and if the persecution is dying down, there shouldn't be a problem.'

'Right then, that's settled. But don't mention it to Thomas yet. He'll only try and persuade us not to go.'

So it was not until the following week, just as the girls were beginning to pack up their belongings, that Margaret mentioned their plans to Thomas. He frowned. 'I don't like the sound of this, Margaret. We've no proof about what Donald said, and I'm sure he would tell you and Agnes to be careful. I'm certainly not going.'

Agnes grinned. 'Scaredy cat!' she said, teasingly, but Thomas didn't laugh.

'Come on, Thomas. If you don't want to come you should just wait here. We'll be back by the evening. Then we can set off to the caves the next day.'

Reluctantly, Thomas agreed to let his sisters go, and the following day he waved them off. Smiling and laughing, Margaret and Agnes felt a spring in their step. Margaret had forgotten how good it felt to walk wherever you wanted, whenever you wanted. It was delicious – the taste of freedom.

Wigton was a good walk from the woods but the girls had set off early so they would get to Margaret MacLachlan's in good time. The roads were quiet on the way into the town and they saw no one to speak to. However, as they drew nearer the centre of the town, a figure emerged from behind an alley way and stopped to stare at them. He was obviously surprised to see them both.

'Margaret and Agnes Wilson, is that you?'

Margaret smiled warmly, 'Yes Patrick, it's been a long time since we've seen you.'

'It has indeed,' he smiled.

Patrick Stuart was a friend of the family, a business

acquaintance of her father and one whom they had known for years.

Patrick continued to ask after her parents, to which Margaret replied that they had been fine the last time she heard. Patrick paused slightly but continued to ask questions, 'How is Thomas? Did you have a good harvest?' and then he asked them, 'Would you like a bit of lunch?'

Margaret looked at Agnes who was slightly uncertain. However, Margaret felt it would be rude to refuse this old family friend so they both agreed to have a bit of lunch with Mr Stuart.

Quickly he ushered them into his little house and laid the table. Then he asked the girls to sit down. Food and drink was laid out. It looked delicious. A cool jug of milk and some freshly baked scones were placed down in front of Agnes. Both girls were very hungry. But they both waited quietly for Patrick to say the blessing on the food. However, Patrick did something else. He reached out and raised his glass. Looking directly at Margaret first and then at Agnes, he cleared his throat. 'A toast to the King,' he proclaimed loudly, before drinking.

Margaret and Agnes were stunned. They hadn't realised that their friend would ask them to do this. A shiver went down Margaret's spine as she realised what she had taken herself and Agnes into. Patrick remained with his glass raised. Then he said it again,

'A toast to the King. Won't you drink the health of our sovereign the King?'

Agnes' hand shook as she placed her glass back on the table. Margaret cleared her throat before adding, 'No, we will not.'

Patrick immediately left them at the table and slammed the outside door. Agnes ran to the window to see where he was going.

'I don't believe it, Margaret, he's running down the street to the Magistrate's house. What are we going to do?'

Margaret grabbed Agnes and pulled her away from the window and through the house to the back door. There was a gate that led to the back alley and they escaped through that.

'Quickly, Agnes, we've got to get out of town before the Magistrate sets the soldiers after us. I thought Donald said the persecution was over?'

Agnes gasped out as she ran, 'It was we who made up our minds it was safe to come. We've only got ourselves to blame.'

'I suppose you're right, but quick – hide. Patrick is back and he's got soldiers with him.'

Margaret and Agnes ducked behind a wall. But it was too late. Patrick had spotted them. They both got up and ran as hard as they could. Calls and shouts went up from the soldiers pursuing them. The girls ran and ran, turning down a road that neither Agnes or Margaret recognised. Too late, they realised that the road they had turned down wasn't a road after all but a dead end.

Margaret stopped and seconds later both she and Agnes were in chains and being dragged along the street to the notorious town prison – The Thieves' Hole.

Before they were thrown in, Margaret turned to look at Patrick Stuart, who had betrayed them. He was receiving his reward of several silver coins from the magistrate – and a pat on the back.

Patrick turned just in time to see Margaret thrown into the hole. His smile said it all. He was no friend of hers.

The Thieves' Hole

When Margaret and Agnes were thrown into the hole, the stench was overwhelming. For decades now, prisoners had been thrown in here to await punishment. There was no heating, food or sanitation. The place stank. It was freezing cold and pitch dark.

In the far corner there was a scuffling noise. Rats, thought Margaret, and she recoiled in disgust. But then a voice was heard, a well-known voice, and Margaret gasped. 'Mrs MacLachlan, is that you? It's Margaret, Margaret Wilson and Agnes.'

A thin, whispery voice sounded out from the far corner of the cell, 'Girls, what are you doing here? I heard you were safe in hiding on the hills. How on earth did they catch you?'

Margaret hung her head in shame. 'It's our own fault really. We should have been more careful. Agnes and I came to Wigton to visit you. We'd heard that the persecution had abated slightly. We thought it would be safe.'

Old Margaret hobbled over to where the girls were and began to soothe Agnes' anxious sobs. 'I heard that rumour too,' she whispered, 'but here I am in jail with yourselves. The winter has certainly been quieter – I haven't heard of any killings since the preacher was hung in Edinburgh. You'll have heard about that?'

'Yes, it's awful.'

'Aye, it is, but the winter was a bad one for everybody. I think it was the cold that kept the soldiers and the magistrates indoors. Now that the spring's here they're ready again to go out persecuting good and righteous people. I'm sorry, though, that you girls are caught up in it. You won't have heard any news of my family? I was arrested at my daughter's house in Drumjargan. We were in the middle of having family worship. I'm the only one they've thrown in here. I don't know if my daughter or her children are alive and well or if they've been thrown in some other jail like me.'

Margaret reached over to comfort her old friend. As the cell grew colder and colder, Margaret realised that the evening must be drawing in. Would Thomas realise that something had happened and raise the alarm? Perhaps he'd be able to get word to her father, or Donald or someone? Right now the only person she could speak to about her problems, the only one who could do anything to help them, was God. So they all knelt and prayed.

Margaret was right about Thomas though. He did realise that something was wrong but there wasn't much he could do about it. As the evening drew in and neither of the girls made an appearance he knew that something was up. Late in the night he decided to pack his bags and make his way to the outskirts of the town to see if he could get any news of what had happened to his two sisters. However, before he got within two miles of the town a figure emerged from behind a hedge giving him the fright of his life. 'Donald! What are you doing here?'

'What are *you* doing here, more's the point? What did you think you were doing, letting your sisters go to Wigton?'

Donald glared at his friend who looked sheepish and confused. 'I told them it was dangerous but they were determined to go now that the persecution has died down.'

Donald groaned. 'I said died down, not stopped! I wouldn't have said anything if I'd thought they were going to charge off at the first opportunity. You won't have heard, Thomas, but they've been betrayed. Margaret and Agnes are in the Thieves' Hole. I've no idea what's going to happen to them. Another old woman is in there with them. Margaret MacLachlan.'

Thomas turned pale. 'Betrayed? By whom? Who would do such a thing?'

'Patrick Stuart, that's who. If I've said it once, I've said it a hundred times, it's the old friends you have to watch out for. It's the quiet ones, the ones you think wouldn't harm a hair on your head. Well, he's got a good share of silver for both of your sisters and he'll be looking out for you next. So you can't go to Wigton. I want you to head for Glenvernock:

tell your father the situation and get him to come and meet me behind the churchyard. Then head for the hills. I don't want to see you back here until all this has died down.'

With that, Thomas turned and ran all the way to Glenvernock. There he woke up his parents and told them the bad news. That very morning, before the sun was up, Gilbert Wilson was on his way to the churchyard to meet up with an unknown outlaw named Donald Mackay. Shaking inwardly with anger, Mr Wilson wished with all his heart that his children had never met up with the Covenanters. 'They've only brought heartache and tragedy to my home... and now my daughters are in jail because of them,' he thought bitterly as he rode.

Tying his horse to a wicket-gate, Mr Wilson walked smartly towards the young man standing at the back of the churchyard. Putting his anger behind him, he discussed the situation with the Covenanter and together they worked out what their next step was to be.

'The authorities will ask the girls to sign the oath,' Donald told Mr Wilson.

'Well, they won't do that,' he growled.

'I know that, Mr Wilson. Your girls are strong Covenanters. They won't give in.'

Mr Wilson's dark eyes darkened even more. Donald knew exactly whom he was blaming for the capture but he didn't say anything about that. He knew how heartbroken Mr Wilson must be feeling. 'The first thing you have to do is to go into town tomorrow and find out how the girls are,' he said gently. 'They are in the Thieves' Hole and you might be able to speak to them, if the Magistrate is agreeable. You have to find out the day of their trial, then we'll try and work out your next step.'

As the sun rose above the hills and began to warm the flats of the Solway Firth, Mr Wilson made his way into the town of Wigton and up to the Magistrate's house. He wasn't allowed to speak to the girls, but he was given the date for their trial. 'Your daughters will be tried before Sir Robert Grierson of Lagg, Colonel David Graham, Major Winram, Captain Strachan and Provost Cultrain at Wigton on the 13th of April, 1685,' he was told.

All Mr Wilson could do was to go back to Glenvernock. His wife would be beside herself with worry. How was he going to tell her that both their young daughters were locked up in the Thieves' Hole? Everyone in the parish of Penninghame knew the story of the place and it was frightening. Before he left the town he went to the jail to ask if he could leave some food for the prisoners. The food was taken but he didn't see the door being opened or any food being given. He wondered if his girls would see any of it.

When the 13th of April arrived, the courtroom was packed. Mr and Mrs Wilson sat near the front. The shock of seeing both their girls shackled in chains took away any joy of seeing them for the first time in months.

'Margaret! Agnes!' Mrs Wilson sobbed.

Margaret turned round, her face pale and anxious. Agnes' eyes were red from crying. Old Mrs MacLachlan was unsteady on her feet. All three looked worn and tired. Margaret quietly whispered to her mother, 'Don't worry, Mother, we're both fine. We'll be fine.'

Agnes turned to Margaret and whispered, 'Can you see Thomas here, or Donald?'

'Don't be foolish, Agnes. Thomas can't come here or Donald either – what if they were spotted? They'd be in this dock after us.' Margaret didn't add that there wasn't much they could do anyway – she wanted to keep Agnes' hopes up and her own. Perhaps there was something that could be done but Margaret now feared the worst.

Then the judges entered the courtroom and the charges were read out.

'The prisoners are charged with the following: being present at the Battles of Bothwell Bridge and Airdsmoss and attendance at numerous field meetings.'

'Well, the first two charges are ridiculous,' muttered Mr Wilson to his wife. 'Agnes was only seven years old at the Battle of Bothwell Bridge; Margaret was only twelve. Mrs MacLachlan would have been well over sixty. None of them could possibly have been at either of these battles. Surely the defence will focus on that and the jury won't let something like that pass.'

However, these facts were not taken into consideration. The defence was woefully inadequate and Donald was certain that the jury had been specially selected.

He met up with Mr and Mrs Wilson later on that night. Ashen-faced, Mrs Wilson stood by the fire in the Glenvernock kitchen.

'I couldn't believe it when the girls and Mrs MacLachlan refused to sign the Abjuration Oath for a second time. And when the men forced them onto their knees to hear the sentence ...' Mrs Wilson sobbed out loud. 'On 11th May 1685 to be tied to a stake fixed within the flood marks in the waters of Bladnoch on the Solway Firth – there to be drowned.' 'My girls, Mr Mackay! My girls are going to die!'

Donald stared at the agonised face of Margaret and Agnes' mother. He had to do something, but what? That night, as he got ready to leave the farm, he turned to speak to Mr Wilson. 'I'll tell you what I can do. I can get news from the girls – I know someone who might be able to get me into the jail.'

Mr Wilson looked at the fiery eyes of the young man in front of him. 'Well, Mackay – getting into jail is one thing. Getting out of it again is another.'

With that, Donald marched out of the farmhouse and disappeared into the night.

Later, muffled sounds were heard within the vicinity of the town jail. A young man with a bushy red beard stood speaking anxiously to Donald in the shadows. 'There's a crack in the wall just by the door. If you're quick about it you'll be able to speak to them for a short time. You've got to go in, then out – no loitering. I'll let you in the back as soon as I start my shift. But you've got to be out before the other guard has finished checking the outside perimeter.'

Donald nodded and handed over a small coin to the bearded man, who turned it away. 'Away with you, man. It's nothing. There are many that don't like this business but we don't have your heart or courage to stand up and do something about it. I wish I could do more for you but my wife, my family – I'm not willing to risk anything.' With that, Donald and the jailer turned the corner and went in through the jailhouse door. Donald flattened himself down against the ground and whispered urgently through the crack. It was very small – hardly big enough for a fly, he thought. Would the girls hear him? He was beginning to doubt if this plan would work.

Agnes was the first to hear something unusual. 'Margaret! It sounds like someone whispering!'

All three listened hard.

'Psst. Psst. It's me – Donald – over here by the wall!'

Margaret shuffled over and crouched down by the wall to hear the urgent whispers.

'Donald, is that you?'

'Yes! I just need to know how you all are. Your parents are worried.'

Agnes squeezed up to the wall too. 'You shouldn't take such risks. What if they find you?'

'Don't worry about me – are you all right?'

Margaret told him everything he needed to know. They were tired and hungry but so far they were keeping warm. God was good and they were gaining encouragement from each other and God's Word.

'Tell Mother that the God who was with Joseph in his prison is with us too. "*God's Word is a comfort to us in affliction and in our difficulties his Word alone revives us.*"'

Donald recognised the words from Psalm 119. Just then, an urgent whistle from the doorway warned him that the guard was on his way. Telling the girls to hold onto their courage, he ran back to the rear of the building and struck out into the night.

Agnes began to sob quietly, but Mrs MacLachlan hushed her. 'Remember that our Lord is always with us – '*he will never leave thee nor forsake thee*'. It says that in Hebrews chapter thirteen so I know it is true. Remember what an honour it is for all of us here to be suffering for the sake of Jesus.'

Margaret hugged Agnes too.

'We should do exactly what Paul and Silas did when they were in prison, Agnes. We should sing psalms.' In the night air, the still, clear voices of the three women rang out strong and true.

'Since better is thy love than life,
my lips thee praise shall give.
I in thy name will lift my hands,
and bless thee while I live.'

As the notes faded, more than one person in Wigton wondered about the faith and strength of the women locked up in the Thieves' Hole. Where did their strength come from, and did they really think that the love of God was better than life?

Margaret certainly did. As she lay down to sleep that night she knew that, despite the errors she had made, the foolishness she had shown in coming to Wigton in the first place, she was in the right place. She was giving honour to her Lord and Saviour Jesus Christ. His love was to her better than her very life. She went to sleep praising his name and seeking his forgiveness.

The Rescuer

Donald returned to the farm to pass on the news about the girls. There was planning to be done and decisions to be made. As Mrs Wilson busied herself in the kitchen, Donald and Mr Wilson made their last plans about Mr Wilson's trip to Edinburgh.

'There's not a lot of time. Remember that if a reprieve is granted it has to come all the way from London. We need all the time we can get. However, as far as Agnes is concerned, the law is on our side.' Mr Wilson listened as he packed the last of his belongings. 'The punishment of death is only for those over sixteen years of age. Agnes should be allowed off, but you'll probably have to pay. Do you have money with you?'

Mr Wilson nodded. 'In my saddle pack – there's a hidden pocket. I've got £100 there.'

Donald whistled. 'That's more than enough, but better to be safe than sorry.'

With that, Mr Wilson shook Donald's hand and looked him in the eye. 'You're a good man, Donald Mackay, and though I blame the Covenanters for bringing this disaster on my home, I won't blame you. You've done all you can to help us since the trial and I now know all that you've done to help our children over the winter. They wouldn't have made it without you.'

Donald smiled. 'Thank you, Mr Wilson, I just hope that I can do a lot more. What I've done is very little and besides, your children have helped me in tricky situations too.'

Mr Wilson turned to his wife before swinging himself up onto the old dapple-grey horse. Donald rode the chestnut mare and together they set off towards Edinburgh. Mrs Wilson waved until they were out of sight. It was the fourteenth of April: another twenty seven days and the Wilson girls and Margaret MacLachlan would be tied to the stake in the Solway Firth.

When Donald and Mr Wilson arrived at the capital city, the courts were hard and unyielding. However, Mr Wilson had gained quite a lot of experience of the court system in the last year and in the end he was able to purchase Agnes' freedom for the princely sum of £100 sterling. Donald was shocked at the news – '£100 sterling, that's all the money you have with you! What will you use to purchase Margaret's freedom?'

Mr Wilson looked pale and anxious. 'I don't know, Donald, I just don't know. But for now I want you to ride as fast as you are able to the court house at Wigton. Don't stop unless your horse is begging for it. Now go, Mackay. Get my child out of the Thieves' Hole!'

Donald immediately did as he was told. He kept his word. He arrived at the court house in Wigton with the reprieve papers in his hand. The Magistrate cast a critical look over them, and had no option but to let Agnes go.

As soon as she stepped out of the prison, Donald lifted her onto the horse and they fled to the hills. He didn't risk taking her back to the farm. Someone could find her there and you didn't trust anyone – not now. Leaving Agnes in the capable hands of Thomas and the other Covenanters, Donald left the caves once again to find out if any news had come from Edinburgh. The days were passing and it wouldn't be long now until Margaret and Mrs MacLachlan would be tied to the stake.

Mrs Wilson was overjoyed to hear that Agnes was now safe with her brother, but she hadn't heard any news from her husband and the time was getting short. Then one day a messenger arrived at the farm. A hurried note had been scribbled onto a piece of paper: 'The prospect of a reprieve from London seems very likely.'

Mrs Wilson counted the days. Could the reprieve really make it in time? She wasn't sure if it would ever materialise, far less make it on time to the courthouse at Wigton.

'The only thing I know for sure is that Margaret will never sign the Abjuration Oath,' she thought desperately. 'A reprieve from the Crown is the only possible way to rescue her from the stake.'

* * * * *

Finally, a reprieve was granted in London on the 30th of April 1685.

The Martyrs

Mr Wilson made haste to the courthouse of Wigton. He passed on the news of the reprieve, but it was met with scorn and ridicule. 'I'll believe it when I see the court seal. You could be making it up – or planning a forgery. Come back when you've more proof.'

By the time the sixth of May came, the Wilsons were getting anxious. Margaret had been allowed to send a letter and in it she sounded very positive. She passed on her love and best wishes, telling them not to worry as she was very conscious of her Saviour's love and God's love for her soul.

'I am reconciled to whatever God has in store for me,' she wrote, but her family and friends struggled on to gain her freedom. Young women, who had grown up with her and played with her as a child, pleaded with Margaret to sign the oath. But no one could persuade her to betray her Saviour, Jesus Christ. She loved him more than anything and anyone.

When the 10th of May came, the reprieve had not arrived. Mr and Mrs Wilson spent all their time in the town pleading with magistrates and officials, even begging Major Winram for mercy. But none was given.

On the 11th of May, early in the morning, the sound was heard of wooden stakes being hammered into the ground. By the afternoon, the tide would have turned and it would be surging up the flats towards the stakes, rising higher and higher.

Later that morning, Margaret Wilson and Margaret MacLachlan were taken from the court house of Wigton to the shores of the Solway Firth, Major Winram himself guarding the procession. One hundred yards from the town, they stopped. In between the low and high water marks two wooden stakes were fastened firmly. They stood about six feet above the level of the sand.

The large crowd of spectators stood in hushed silence. Margaret Wilson and Margaret MacLachlan stood dignified as the scene unfolded before them. The soldiers advanced, and at the orders of Major Winram, Margaret MacLachlan was taken and tied firmly to the stake nearest the water. Instructions to tie the woman tightly were obeyed without question.

'We want the young lassie to see her drown. That might frighten her into changing her mind. We'll soon see how brave she is,' taunted the commander.

Many of the people looking on couldn't believe what was actually happening. Many had thought that it would never go this far ... but it had. The days had passed and the law had remained unyielding. No one had spoken out. Nobody was willing to stick their necks out or to take a stand. Too many were frightened for their own lives. Very few people in Wigton that day had the courage, conviction or dignity of the two women being tied to the stake.

As the tide turned and the waves flooded in, Margaret MacLachlan's waist was soon covered by the advancing tide. Each wave brought the water higher and higher – her waist, her chest, now she strained her neck to get away from the advancing waters. Would she change her mind? No. Margaret MacLachlan, an old widow of over sixty years of age, stood firm as the cold waters lapped at her neck – then covered her mouth. It was over. The eyes of the crowd now turned to Margaret Wilson.

Margaret moaned slightly as she witnessed the last moments of her friend's life. Soldiers on the side-lines were laughing. The Major, mounted on his horse beside her, sneered as he saw her pale face and wide eyes, 'What do you think of that?' he called out to Margaret as the first waves began to lap around her feet.

'What do I see?' she said calmly. 'I see Christ, in one of his people suffering. He sends none into the battle on their own.' Margaret whispered the verses that gave her the most comfort, '*Come, ye blessed of my Father, inherit the kingdom prepared for you from the foundation of the world.*' That's where she is now,' Margaret sighed as she saw the soldiers raising the old woman's head to check that she was really dead. 'She is with you, Jesus, and I am coming – I am ready for you to take me.'

The tide progressed steadily and soon the water was creeping up her legs. And as the water came closer, friends and neighbours called out to her, 'Sign the oath, Margaret! Just sign it! It's just words, that's all.'

'Dear girl, please! Just sign it.'

'Have courage, Margaret. Be strong!' another voice called out.

As the waters advanced further, Margaret's clear, strong, voice began to sing once again.

> 'My sins and faults of youth
> do thou, O Lord forget,
> After thy mercy think on me,
> and for thy goodness great.
>
> God good and upright is:
> the way he'll sinners show.
> The meek in judgement he will guide,
> and make his path to know.'

Then, with a calm and cheerful voice, she called out above the anxious voices and the sounds of the jeering soldiers,

> 'Who shall separate us from the love of Christ?
> Shall tribulation, or distress, or persecution, or famine,
> or nakedness, or peril, or sword? As it is written,
> For thy sake we are killed all the day long; we are
> accounted as thy sheep for the slaughter.
> Nay, in all these things we are more than conquerors
> through him that loved us.

For I am persuaded, that neither death, nor life,
nor angels, nor principalities, nor powers,
nor things present, nor things to come,
nor height, nor depth, nor any other creature,
shall be able to separate us from the love of God,
which is in Christ Jesus our Lord.'

Throughout this passage the waters had advanced, quickly gaining momentum as they neared the shore. Before the waters reached her lips, Margaret began to pray. Just then the soldiers cut her free. A huge sigh of relief was heard from the crowd.

'I knew they wouldn't go through with it,' a young woman exclaimed.

But a rough soldier held Margaret by the hair just above the water. Margaret gasped and struggled for breath as he yelled in her face, 'Will you pray for the king?'

Margaret gasped, 'I wish the salvation of all men and damnation of none.'

'Margaret, Margaret!' a young woman called out from the shore. 'Say, God save the king. Please, say God save the king!'

Margaret, composed, replied, 'God save him, if he will, for it is his salvation that I desire.'

Immediately after that, the young woman swung round to Major Winram who was watching the proceedings. 'There, she has said it. She has said it. Let her go now!'

But none of the king's men was satisfied with Margaret's statement.

Grierson of Lagg cursed her. He was well-known for his evil temper. 'We don't want that wench's prayers. Make her sign the oath!'

Winram rode his mount into the Solway Firth and came right up to Margaret, who was straining her head above the waters. The waves swelled towards her, the salty water choking her as it surged through her nostrils and down her throat.

'Swear the Abjuration Oath or else you will be immediately tied up again in the sea.'

There was no hesitation as Margaret turned to look him in the face.

'I will not. I am one of Christ's children; let me go.'

Soldiers quickly re-tied her to the stake. Then the town officer took his spear and with the blunt end shoved Margaret gleefully back into the water. 'Take another drink then,' he exclaimed, chuckling.

The crowd on the shores wept in shock and horror at what they were witnessing. The waters swirled around the stake advancing higher and higher. Soon the waters covered her. A mass of chestnut hair floated on the surface and then vanished. Margaret Wilson was the second Wigton Martyr – drowned at the stake for the crime of following Christ.

***

'And that's the truth of it ...' Donald stood by the fire in the chilly little farmer's cottage beside the anxious, bewildered faces of the Covenanters. 'There's not much to add to the story. Some say that Margaret

MacLachlan wrote a letter saying that she would sign the oath but that she repented at the last minute and wouldn't do it, but I don't believe it. For as long as I can remember that woman could never string as much as two words together. She certainly couldn't have written that letter as some say that she did. It was probably well-meaning relatives trying to get her free. Margaret Wilson, though, never faltered. To the very end, she stood firm. I'll never forget her and neither should you.'

'No, Donald, we won't forget. We owe it to her. If her people were to forget what she and others went through ...' the voice stopped short. The very idea that people would forget the tragedy was unbelievable.

It had been a few years now but Donald would always keep Margaret's story in the memory of these people. She deserved that at least. There were still persecutions and people were still scorned and belittled for following Christ. Perhaps they always would be? After all, Jesus Christ had said in his Word that the world would always hate those who loved him. However, Donald hoped that in the future they would see the day when ordinary people would be able to worship God in peace and freedom once more.

A woman clutching a young child turned to Donald and asked, 'What about the others – Thomas, Agnes, the parents?'

'Mr Wilson died in poverty and his widow was left penniless. Thomas left to join the army – no one has heard of him since. Agnes… well, not many people know where she is but I hope she's safe.'

Then, in the light of the fire, the Covenanters left the story of the Wigton martyrs for another day. Donald was left to his own thoughts, thoughts of the young woman waiting for him at home, the tragedy they both shared and the memory they both cherished of a godly young girl who would not give in.

'Agnes misses Margaret so much,' Donald thought, as he knelt a little closer to the fire and thought about his own refuge in the hills and his young family. It was there that his young and sorrowful wife kept far away from Wigton, from Glenvernock and from anyone who might remember who she was.

Margaret was no longer here. But others who had known and loved her struggled on, keeping her memory alive and keeping the faith that she had died for.

'They didn't have to kill her,' Donald thought sadly, 'but she had to make that stand. She knew that the love of God was better than life – and she followed him to the end.'

Margaret Wilson – Who was she?

The years of 1684 and 1685 were called the 'Killing Years.' It was a time of great change for the nation of Scotland, and centuries after that time the world still owes a great debt to the people known as Covenanters. But who were they and what did they do?

The Covenanters were men, women and children who stood against the dictatorship of their day and demanded a basic freedom that people in Scotland now take for granted. They demanded freedom of worship and for this demand many died.

Some were executed and murdered by the king's authorities because they believed that Jesus Christ was the head of the church. With God's Word for their guide they looked at the monarchy of their land and saw a system that was contrary to God's law. King Charles II set himself up as the head of the church and people were ordered to sign an oath that acknowledged the monarch as the head of the church – and not Christ. This was the oath Margaret Wilson refused to sign.

This story really happened. There are monuments in Wigton to Margaret Wilson. When you stand at the Solway Firth and watch the tide rising you realise a little of what it must have been like for the eighteen-year-old looking on as the waters drowned her friend.

Not many facts are known about the case, however. The details are very basic. We don't know what

Margaret looked like, we don't know much about where she lived or about what her parents actually felt about their children following the Covenanters. We do know that they didn't belong to the group themselves, so we can guess that things must have been difficult in young Margaret's home. However, the story you will have read in this book is based on facts, researched and recorded by Christians throughout the years. We don't know what Margaret herself thought about many of the experiences and difficulties that she went through. We only know that she loved her Lord Jesus Christ so much that she was willing to follow him to the very last, even if it meant death.

Margaret's father really did die in poverty and her mother was left penniless. Archive material shows that Thomas is believed to have joined the army. Nothing more was ever heard of him. Nothing at all is known of what happened to Agnes, but it is good to imagine that she did find safety at last; perhaps with someone like Donald Mackay, perhaps with other friends who could keep her secret and keep her safe.

Christian martyrs are not only from the past. The last 100 years have seen more Christian martyrs throughout the world than the whole of the last 2,000 years. That is why Margaret's story should be remembered. Her story tells us that following Christ is costly, but that it is worthless to gain the whole world yet lose your own soul!

Margaret Wilson Timeline

1603	Death of Elizabeth I. Ascension of James VI of Scotland as James I of England.
1604	**Publishing:** First English dictionary by Robert Cawdrey, *A Table Alphabeticall*.
1605	**Politics:** 5th November. Gunpowder Plot. An attempt is made to blow up King James and the Parliament.
1608	**Science:** First telescope invented.
1609	**Media:** The first regular newspaper is published in Germany.
1611	**Church:** 'Authorized' (King James) version of the Bible published.
1616	**Literature:** Death of William Shakespeare.
1620	**America:** The Pilgrim Fathers depart for America in the Mayflower and land at Plymouth in Massachusetts.
1625	Death of James I. Accession of Charles I.
1628	**Politics:** Oliver Cromwell joins parliament.
1632	**Art:** Birth of (Sir) Christopher Wren, architect.
1636	**Education:** First university in North America: Harvard College.
1638	Birth of the future Louis XIV of France.
1640	**Invention:** First cinema projector is invented by Kirchner.

1642	The English Civil War begins.
	Science: Birth of (Sir) Isaac Newton, scientist.
1643	Death of Louis XIII of France.
	Church: Westminster Assembly meets for the first time.
1644	**China:** Manchus founds Ch'ing dynasty.
1646	**Church:** Publication of the Westminster Confession of Faith.
1648	**Church:** Publication of the Longer and Shorter Catechisms.
1649	**Politics:** Trial and execution of Charles I; establishment of the Commonwealth under Oliver Cromwell's leadership.
1658	Oliver Cromwell dies.
1659	**Finance:** First cheque is drawn in London on 6th February.
1666	**Events:** Great Fire of London (city destroyed).
	Science: Newton's Laws of Gravitation.
1682	**Russia:** Accession of Czar Peter the Great.
1685	*Margaret Wilson tried for treason.*
	Music: G.F. Handel born in Halle.
	Music: J.S. Bach born in Eisenach.
1688	Arrival of William and Mary as King and Queen from the Netherlands.
1689	**Politics:** Declaration of Rights. Establishment of Constitutional monarchy in England.
1694	**Finance:** Establishment of the Bank of England.

Take Five Minutes ...

Take five minutes and think: Why did Margaret Wilson die? Was it just because wicked people killed her or is there another reason?

Margaret Wilson died because she loved Jesus Christ most. She was asked to sign the Abjuration Oath which gave the king more importance than Jesus Christ. This was something she could not and would not do.

Margaret knew what she was doing. She understood that she could be put to death, but that it was an honour to suffer for Jesus Christ. She knew that Jesus Christ had suffered and died to bring her salvation. She knew that when she died she would go to heaven to be with him. Jesus suffered more than any person ever did or ever will suffer. Margaret was overjoyed to suffer and die in order to bring glory and honour to God.

Our sufferings too can bring glory to God. If we trust and follow him, when we suffer we can show people that faith in the one true God can make all the difference. He is like a strong tower to which we can run for safety. We will still have troubles, but we will be certain that in the end, God's people will be with him. Everlasting life is a promise from God to those who follow him. God always keeps his promises.

Bible Study 1

Look up the following chapters:
John 19:17-37
Luke 23:26-49
Mark 15:21-41

These verses tell us something of the suffering of Jesus Christ. Look through these verses and find the seven different things that Jesus said while he was hanging on the cross.

Underline where you see him suffering:
a) physically
b) emotionally
c) spiritually

Mark in your Bible where you see Jesus caring for others, even though he is suffering greatly.

From whom is Jesus separated in Mark 15:34? He is separated because he has become sin for us, as it says in 2 Corinthians 5:21. This shows us that Jesus has suffered more than anyone ever has or ever will.

Take Five Minutes ...

Around the world today, Christians are killed and hated because of their faith in Jesus Christ. Why?

Jesus said that his followers would be hated by the non-believing world because the world hated him. In fact, it would be strange to think of the world not hating Christians when it hated their leader so much that he was tortured to death.

Jesus stands for everything that the world hates. He is the Son of God. Jesus is perfect and sinless. He shows people their sin through his Word and his life. People do not like to be told that they are wrong. It is only when God works in a person's heart that that person realises they are sinful, and that they have to ask God for his help and forgiveness.

Those whose hearts are still hard and hateful against God and his truth, are often hard and hateful against people who love God and who have given their lives to him. In some instances, this means that Christians are killed. In other instances, it means that they are bullied or made fun of. Jesus knows what it is like – he was bullied, made fun of and eventually killed. But he came back to life and that gives all Christians a certain hope of eternal life.

Bible Study 2

Look up the following chapter:
Psalm 91

This chapter is still relevant to God's people today when we are in trouble.

1. Write down all the things in verses 3-10 that God protects us from.

2. God protects us from small things as well as big things. What does God protect you from in verse 12?

3. What animals are mentioned in this psalm?

4. What animal is God described as in verse 4?

5. What building is God described as in verse 2?

6. What is God's reason in verse 14 for protecting us?

7. Read the last verse of this psalm. What is the best protection that God can give us?

Take Five Minutes ...

What do you think about the word 'freedom'? Does it mean that we can do exactly what we like?

The best freedom is the freedom that comes from God – a freedom to obey him. As his law is perfect, following his instructions is the best way to live our lives. If we ignore God's instructions we may think that this is freedom - but the ultimate result is an eternity of death in hell, where freedom has no meaning at all.

In many places today, people do what they like regardless of the pain that it causes others. Christians have their 'freedom' taken away because other people are free to kill and persecute them. In some countries there is religious freedom. Christians are free to worship God without fear. This is a gift from God and we should thank him for it. It is because Christians in the past have suffered and died that we have this freedom.

There are young people today who can now read the Bible freely and in their own language, because other Christians stood up for Jesus Christ. We should pray this will be true for young people of the future too. This freedom is a gift given to us because of the grace and love of God.

Bible Study 3

Look up the following chapter:
Exodus 20:1-17

Many people look on these verses as a list of things that they should not do. They think that God's commandments are just there so that they won't have a good time.

1. How does verse 2 show that God cares about people?

2. How does verse 8 show that God has our best interests at heart?

3. How does verse 12 show that God cares about our families and relationships?

4. How many of these commandments are directly connected with God? (i.e. worshipping him alone; honouring him.)

5. How many of these commandments are directly connected to human beings? (i.e. our relationships with other people; our personal lives.)

Take Five Minutes ...

What would you do if you had to face persecution like Margaret? How do you deal with people who are cruel or nasty to you?

Did you know that the 20th century was the most violent century the world has ever known? In countries such as Burma, Indonesia and Saudi Arabia Christians were, and still can be killed for their beliefs.

In other countries, Christians are free to worship God, but people still despise them. Christians can be made fun of. If they want to keep Sunday as a special day for God it can be difficult for them to play in competitive sports. Read about Eric Liddell in 'Ten Boys who changed the World' by Irene Howat. Eric faced persecution for keeping God's day, and years later he was killed in a Japanese prisoner-of-war camp because he loved Jesus and followed him.

We should pray and do all we can to support Christians in countries where persecution is rife. Pray that God would support them and you when facing these trials.

Bible Study 4

Look up the following chapters:
Acts 6:8-15; 7:54-60; 8:1-4

These verses tell us about the first Christian martyr
– Stephen.

1. What was special about Stephen? Acts 6:8

2. What happens to Stephen in Acts 6:9?

3. Who was Stephen's helper in verse 10?

4. Read John 14:15-17. Who else spoke about
   sending this helper?

5. Which one of the ten commandments did
   Stephen's accusers break in Acts 6:13?

6. Which one of the ten commandments did they
   falsely accuse Stephen of breaking?

7. What did Stephen say in Acts 7:60? Look up
   Luke 23:34. Who else said words like Stephen's?

Take Five Minutes ...

Margaret Wilson prayed for the king who persecuted her. Do you pray for people who have been cruel to you?

The Bible tells us to pray for and bless those who persecute us (Matthew 5:44; Romans 12:14). We may want revenge when someone hurts us, but God says we should live peaceably with people. God says that he will avenge and he will repay. God also says that all have sinned. That includes you and me. Christians are sinners too. Even though they love God and try to follow him, they are not perfect. God knows all our sin and he is always willing to forgive those who ask him. That might include the person who is persecuting you. One of the worst persecutors the church has ever known was Saul, who became the apostle Paul after his conversion.

Perhaps countries where Christians are being killed today will, one day, be countries where Jesus is loved and worshipped freely. Perhaps the person who is cruel to you will one day ask God to forgive them. But we should make sure that we have asked God to forgive us. Even as Christians we should always ask God to forgive our sins. He is ready and willing to do this.

Bible Study 5

Look up the following chapter:
Luke 6:27-36

1. In verses 27 and 28 we are told to pray and do good things for four types of people. Who are they?

2. What are we supposed to do when someone physically hurts us? (Verse 29)

3. What are we supposed to do when someone steals from us? (Verses 29 and 30)

4. To whom is God kind? (Verse 35)

5. If we give things to people without expecting anything in return, what can we expect from God? (Verse 35)

Answers: Bible Study 1

Answers – Seven sayings of Christ on the Cross – Mark 15:34; Luke 23:34; 23:43; 23:46; John 19:26-27; 19-28; 19:30.

Examples of physical suffering: Crucifixion, thirst. *Examples of emotional suffering*: the rulers sneered at him; the soldiers mocked him; the criminal insulted him. *Example of spiritual suffering*: God abandoned him. *Where Jesus cares for others*: he cares for his mother; he cares for the thief on the cross. *Who he is separated from*: He is separated from God.

Bible Study 2

Answers – **1.** Fowler's snare; deadly pestilence; terror by night; arrow that flies by day; pestilence; plague; harm; disaster. **2.** Tripping over a stone. **3.** Lion, adder, young lion, dragon. **4.** A bird. **5.** A fortress. **6.** Because he loves us. **7.** Salvation.

Bible Study 3

Answers – 1 He rescued them from slavery in Egypt. **2.** He gives us a day of rest. **3.** We are told to honour our parents. **4.** The first three commandments are connected to the worship and honouring of God, the fourth commandment is linked to God in that it is a day set aside for worshipping him. **5.** Commandments connected to human beings. The fourth: Rest is a gift from God to us. The fifth: We are told to honour our parents. The sixth: We are told not to kill other people.

The seventh: We are told not to commit adultery or to cheat on our husband or wife. The eighth: We are told not to steal from other people. The ninth: We are told not to tell lies about other people. The tenth: We are told not to be jealous of or covet other people's possessions.

Bible Study 4
Answers – **1.** He was a man full of God's grace and power and he did great things and miracles for all to see. (Acts 6:8) **2.** People opposed him and argued with him. **3.** The Holy Spirit. **4.** Jesus Christ. **5.** The ninth commandment. **6.** The third commandment. **7.** He asked God to forgive his enemies. Jesus Christ also asked God to do this when he was being crucified.

Bible Study 5
Answers – **1.** Enemies; those who hate us; those who curse us; those who ill-treat us. **2.** If someone hits us we shouldn't hit back, but we should 'Turn the other cheek' – that means we shouldn't try and stop them. It is exactly the opposite to what we would normally want to do. This shows how different Jesus Christ and his followers are to the non-believing world. **3.** When someone steals our coat we aren't supposed to stop them. **4.** God is kind to the ungrateful and the wicked. **5.** A reward.

CHRISTIAN FOCUS PUBLICATIONS

Christian Focus | Christian Heritage | CF4K | Mentor

Christian Focus Publications publishes books for adults and children under its four main imprints: Christian Focus, CF4K, Mentor and Christian Heritage. Our books reflect our conviction that God's Word is reliable and Jesus is the way to know him, and live for ever with him.

Our children's publication list includes a Sunday School curriculum that covers pre-school to early teens, and puzzle and activity books. We also publish personal and family devotional titles, biographies and inspirational stories that children will love.

If you are looking for quality Bible teaching for children then we have an excellent range of Bible stories and age-specific theological books.

From pre-school board books to teenage apologetics, we have it covered!

Find us at our web page:
www.christianfocus.com

CF4•K
Because you're never too young to know Jesus